Fun With Fiber™

Edited by Vicki Blizzard

Annie's Attic®

CONTENTS

Staff
Editor: Vicki Blizzard
Associate Editor: Tanya Fox
Copy Editors: Michelle Beck, Conor Allen
Technical Editor: Brooke Smith
Technical Artist: Brooke Smith
Graphic Arts Supervisor: Ronda Bechinski
Graphic Artist: Dan Kraner
Photography: Tammy Christian, Carl Clark, Christena Green
Photo Stylist: Tammy Nussbaum

Annie's Attic®

306 East Parr Road, Berne, IN 46711
©2005 Annie's Attic

TOLL-FREE ORDER LINE or to request
a free catalog (800) 582-6643
Customer Service (800) 282-6643,
Fax (800) 882-6643
Pattern Services (260) 589-4000, ext. 333

Visit www.AnniesAttic.com

Fun With Fiber is published by Annie's Attic, 306 East Parr
Road, Berne, IN 46711, telephone (260) 589-4000. Printed in
USA. Copyright © 2005 Annie's Attic.
RETAILERS: If you would like to carry this pattern book
or any other Annie's Attic publications, call the Wholesale
Department at Annie's Attic to set up a direct account:
(903) 636-4303. Toll-free order line or to request a free
catalog (800) LV-ANNIE (800-582-6643). Customer Service:
(800) AT-ANNIE (800-282-6643), Fax (800) 882-6643. Also,
request a complete listing of publications available from
Annie's Attic. Visit www.AnniesAttic.com.

ISBN: 1-59635-003-2
Library of Congress: 2004116277

1 2 3 4 5 6 7 8 9

I've become a fiber-aholic! Everywhere I go, I collect little bits and pieces of yarn and string to use in my paper crafts. Nothing is too small— even a two-inch piece of plain string is still long enough to hold a few beads and attach to the front of a card. I now have bags filled with little snippets of fashion yarns, organdy ribbons, metallic braids and, of course, string.

My family laughed at me at first, but now they are on the lookout for scraps of fibers to add to my collection. After all, they are the ones who receive the unique projects that are created using them!

My love of fiber is what inspired the concept for this book. Our designers have created some very unique ways to incorporate interesting fibers into paper crafts, and I know

you'll find the perfect project here to use some of those fun fiber scraps that you have been accumulating, too!

Warm regards,

Vicki Blizzard

Dance Tag

Design by SAHILY GONZALEZ

The muted background colors draw attention to the striking black and white photo that celebrates the dance.

Cut a 5½-inch square from ivory card stock; cut a 2 x 5½-inch strip of green floral-print paper and adhere on top portion of square. Cut a 3½ x 5½-inch rectangle from pink paper and adhere to bottom portion of square. Apply brown ink to edges.

Use a computer to print a dance image onto canvas paper. ***Note:*** *A black and white dance image not printed on a computer may also be used.* Glue dance photo in bottom right corner.

Apply brown and pink ink to the edges of the "dance" definition sticker and attach alongside dance image. Use alphabet rubber stamps and brown ink to stamp "poetry" onto square referring to photo for placement. Finish quote by handwriting the rest of the following: "dancing is the poetry of the soul" with a brown fine-tip pen. Emboss metal embellishment using watermark ink pad and pink embossing powder; adhere to square. Punch a hole at top and thread fibers through. ∎

SOURCES: Green floral-print paper from Chatterbox; sticker and metal word embellishment from Making Memories; PSX alphabet rubber stamps from Duncan.

MATERIALS

Ivory card stock
Pink paper
Green floral-print paper
Pink and green fibers
"Dance" definition sticker
"Dance" metal embellishment
Dance image
Canvas paper
Pink embossing powder
Brown and pink ink pads
Watermark ink pad
Alphabet rubber stamps
Brown fine-tip pen
Glue stick
Adhesive dots
Heat embossing tool
Hole punch
Computer and scanner
 (optional)

Around the World Centerpiece

Design by MARY LYNN MALONEY, *courtesy of Krylon*

Create a unique centerpiece for a den or library. The paper-wrapped balls are reminiscent of world globes.

MATERIALS

Plastic foam shapes: 2
  (4-inch diameter) and
  3 (3-inch diameter)
  balls and 1 (10-inch
  diameter) hollow half
  ball
18 x 24-inch sheet multi-
  colored lightweight
  handmade paper
3 (18 x 24-inch) old world
  map-print patterned
  papers
2 yards multi-color fibers
Copper leafing pen
Foam setting medium
Acrylic adhesive medium
Fabric adhesive
Serrated knife
4 to 5 pairs of disposable
  latex gloves
Baking parchment paper
Large plastic bowl
Water

Project note: *Drying time is very important in this project, so plan accordingly.*

To form the bowl, use the serrated knife to carefully cut off the rounded portion of the 10-inch diameter half ball so it will sit flat on a table. Put on latex gloves and use hands to spread a thin, even layer of foam setting medium inside bowl and halfway down the outside; let dry completely. Turn bowl over and finish applying setting medium to remaining areas. Cover plastic foam balls in same manner allowing them to dry on parchment paper.

In a large plastic bowl, mix acrylic adhesive medium with water at a two-to-one ratio. Tear multi-colored handmade paper into various-sized strips. Cover work surface with a large sheet of backing parchment and put on a clean pair of latex gloves. Dip strips of paper into glue and water mixture; apply randomly onto bowl. Use fingers to smooth more mixture onto paper strips. Continue process covering the inside of the bowl and halfway down the outside; set aside to dry. Turn bowl over and repeat process to cover the remaining areas; let dry.

Tear the old world map papers into strips. Put on a clean pair of latex gloves; follow same procedure as above to cover the plastic foam balls with the map paper strips. Let dry completely.

Tear narrow strips of map paper and use same gluing procedure to apply strips around the upper edge of bowl just below rim; let dry. Apply random areas of color to rim of bowl using copper leafing pen; let dry.

Run a thin line of fabric adhesive around the diameter of one of the large plastic foam balls; adhere multi-colored fiber to line and trim any excess. Repeat process on remaining plastic foam balls. Let each dry thoroughly and place in bowl. ∎

SOURCES: Plastic foam shapes from Dow Chemical Co.; Foam Finish and Fabri-Tac adhesive from Beacon; copper leafing pen from Krylon; Perfect Paper Adhesive from USArtQuest.

Postage Stamp Bookmark

Design by KATHY WEGNER

Gently remove cancelled postage stamps from your mail and recycle them into a fun bookmark with a tropical look!

MATERIALS

- 2 x 6-inch orange card stock
- 3 small used fruit postage stamps
- Green ink pad
- 1¼-inch square sponge
- Black fine-tip permanent marker
- Orange and yellow fibers
- ¼-inch hole punch
- Paper adhesive
- Container filled with warm water
- Paper towel
- Wax paper

Project note: To loosen glue and paper from used stamps, soak postage stamps in warm water for 10 minutes. Blot stamps onto paper towel; let dry on wax paper.

Sponge three squares evenly spaced vertically onto orange card stock; let dry. Draw black wavy lines around squares; adhere postage stamps inside squares. Punch hole at top of card stock. Cut several 12-inch pieces of fibers. Fold fibers in half and thread through hole; pull fiber ends through formed loop. Trim ends. ∎

Summer Fun Frame

Design by SUSAN STRINGFELLOW

Surround your favorite beach vacation photo with water-like printed papers. A few strands of sparkling fibers and wire add a buried treasure look!

Tear pieces of blue and green patterned papers; use glue stick to adhere them to frame overlapping edges until frame is completely covered. Cut a 2½-inch-long strip of vellum with summer-themed words printed on it; apply black solvent-based ink to edges of strip and attach in top right corner of frame. Cut a 2½ x 2-inch piece of vellum; add black ink to edges and attach in bottom left corner. Attach a blue rhinestone in each corner of frame with craft glue. Cut five 7-inch lengths of fibers; twist them together and attach them 1 inch from frame bottom. Attach swirl clip to fibers. ■

SOURCES: Patterned papers from NRN Designs; vellum from EK Success; rhinestones from Hirschberg Schutz & Co.; swirl clip from Making Memories; solvent-based ink pad from Tsukineko.

MATERIALS

5 x 7-inch papier-mâché frame
Blue and green patterned papers
Summer-themed words printed vellum
Silver and blue fibers
Blue rhinestone studs
Spiral clip
Black solvent-based ink pad
Glue stick
Craft glue

Boudoir Paper Basket

Design by BARBARA MATTHIESSEN

Here's an interesting use of both paper tape and fuzzy fibers. This basket will be right at home in a trendy teen's room!

MATERIALS

- 22 yards 2-inch-wide pre-creased sheetrock paper tape
- Gold metallic spray paint
- Translucent spray paint: red, yellow and purple
- Gold webbing spray
- Eyelash fibers: pink, red and purple
- Single strand gold cord
- Instant-dry paper adhesive
- Yarn needle
- Clothespins
- Tape measure

Cut twenty-two 36-inch-long strips of sheetrock tape; place strips, unfolded, onto a protected work surface outdoors. Following manufacturer's instructions, spray all strips randomly with all three translucent paints and gold metallic paint. Allow strips to dry thoroughly. Lightly spray gold webbing onto strips; allow strips to dry.

Fold each strip in half along crease with painted sides facing out. Place six strips side by side on a flat work surface; weave six strips across these strips in a basket weave. Slide strips close together making sure ends are even side to side. Apply dots of paper adhesive between strip layers where they intersect.

Begin to weave basket sides by bending strips up from the base square and weaving strips in a basket weave. Use clothespins to help hold strips in place. Glue strip ends inside basket as each strip is woven through. Continue to weave until eight rows have been completed.

Fold inside strips over to the outside and glue to secure; allow glue to set and then trim excess. Fold outside strips over to inside; glue to secure and allow to dry before trimming excess. Place a strip over the top row along both the inside and outside edges to form a sandwich; use clothespins to hold in place. Overlap ends and glue.

Thread yarn needle with two yards of single strand gold cord; overhand stitch the top rim strip to basket by running needle between woven strips in top row, over top of rim strip and then back between woven strips. Continue process along entire rim; knot off cord. Repeat working in opposite direction all the way around; repeat a third time using two fiber strands.

Thread additional fibers and cord through stitches beginning in one corner leaving random lengths to hang down sides. Continue all the way around; knot in corner and allow ends to hang. Repeat four times with cord and 10 times with fibers. ∎

SOURCES: Spray paints and webbing spray from Krylon; Zip Dry paper adhesive from Beacon.

Friendship Book

Design by SARA NAUMANN, *courtesy of Hot Off The Press*

Carry a theme through the pages of a friendship book by accenting pages with the same fibers used on the cover.

MATERIALS

5 x 7-inch blank book kit
Assorted neutral and
brown papers
Ivory parchment paper
Assorted tag and word
embellishments
Friendship sentiments
Ivory fibers
Assorted brads
Tan and pink chalk
Brown ink pad
¼-inch hole punch
Adhesive foam tape
Glue stick
Tape

Cut a 6 x 8-inch piece of brown paper and adhere to center of front book cover. Miter cut the corners and fold each at a 45 degree angle; glue in place. Punch holes at left side of cover; repeat process for back cover.

Cut a 5½ x 3½-inch piece of ivory parchment paper; crumple up and unfold carefully. Apply brown ink over random areas of crumpled paper. Tear out desired friendship sentiment; apply pink chalk lightly over sentiment. Apply brown ink to edges and adhere onto a piece of brown paper. Trim edges. Place two small gold brads at top of piece. Center and adhere matted sentiment onto crumpled paper; attach a tag embellishment in bottom right corner. Wrap fibers around cover securing ends inside; adhere assembled piece to cover.

Continue to layer papers together on each page and embellish as desired with fibers, brads, sentiments,

etc. Once all pages are completed, line up pages and front and back covers. Cut three 18-inch lengths of fibers. Place them in three separate groups with each group having six fibers. Gather one group and wrap a small piece of tape around the ends. Beginning with the center hole pull the fibers through all the pages; tie a loose knot. Repeat for remaining two holes. Carefully take tape off fiber ends. ∎

SOURCES: Blank book kit, fibers, papers, brads, friendship sentiments and embellishments from Hot Off The Press.

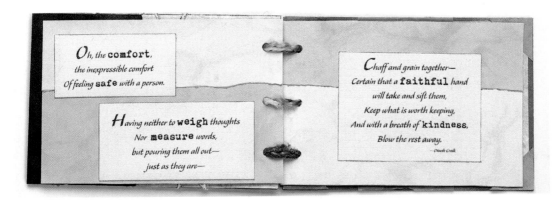

Gardening Girl Tag

Design by KATHLEEN PANEITZ

Pink-ball chain adds a shiny touch to this metal-embellished tag.

Cut a tag shape from pale green card stock; tear a piece of floral patterned paper and adhere down left side of tag. Trim edge if necessary. Tear a piece of cork paper; adhere to top of tag and trim edges. Punch a square from pink card stock and attach at center top of tag; attach square eyelet through pink square. Thread fibers through eyelet and tie.

Stamp the watering can image onto silver metallic paper with black ink; emboss with clear embossing powder. Carefully cut out image; cut small inside areas with a craft knife. Adhere to tag at an angle.

Use a computer or hand-print "gardening" onto cream card stock; attach metal eyelet frame over word using small green brads. Trim card stock around tag. Cut a thin strip of pink card stock and adhere across bottom of tag; attach metal frame vertically over pink strip.

Punch a large square from cork paper; attach a metal alphabet charm to cork square. Adhere on top of pink strip. Use rub-on transfer to apply the word "girl" to pink card stock; cut a rectangle around word and apply pink ink to edges. Set white flower eyelet on one end of rectangle and thread pink metal chain through eyelet. Hang chain from fibers at top of tag.

Add small garden charms with white mini brads and apply pink ink to edges of tag. ■

SOURCES: PSX paper from Duncan; rub-on transfers, metal eyelet frame tag and alphabet charms from Making Memories; rubber stamp from Wordsworth; eyelets from Creative Impressions and Creative Imaginations; brads from Magic Scraps and Doodlebug Designs; pink metal chain from Impress Rubber Stamps.

MATERIALS

Pink floral patterned paper
Silver metallic paper
Card stock: cream,
pale green and pink
Alphabet rub-on transfers
Silver metal eyelet frame
Silver alphabet square charm
Watering can rubber stamp
Black and dark pink ink pads
Clear embossing powder
White flower eyelet
Large decorative square eyelet
2 white mini round brads
4 small green brads
Pink and green fibers
Pink metal chain
Spade and trowel garden charms
Square punch
Hole punch
Paper adhesive
Metal adhesive
Heat tool
Craft knife
Computer font (optional)

Butterfly Card & Gift Bag Set DIAGRAM ON PAGE 93

Design by HELEN RAFSON

Accent corrugated butterflies with variegated embroidery floss and add a springtime touch to your gift giving!

Card

Use pattern to trace butterfly onto the backside of corrugated paper; cut out. Mark dots ⅛ inch from edge between ridges along the entire perimeter of butterfly. Refer to photo as reference. Make holes through dots with sewing needle. Thread needle with olive green floss; knot end and make straight stitches between dots on butterfly body. Secure ends in back with instant-hold glue; let dry.

Thread needle with variegated pink floss. Starting at one end of upper wing section, stitch straight stitches between dots; secure ends in back. Thread needle with variegated purple floss. Starting at one end of lower wing section, stitch straight stitches between dots; secure ends in back. Refer to photo throughout.

Cut a 3⅛-inch piece of black craft wire; bend wire in half and curl ends. Glue wire to back of butterfly head with paper adhesive; let dry.

Adhere butterfly to card front and draw stitch marks around perimeter with black fine-tip pen. Punch six butterflies from pink card stock and six butterflies from purple card stock; glue butterflies randomly onto card. Adhere "imagine" wire word in lower right corner; let dry.

Gift Bag

Make butterfly as directed above and adhere to gift bag. Draw stitch marks around perimeter of bag with black fine-tip marker. Use butterfly punch to punch two butterflies from pink card stock and two butterflies from purple card stock; adhere to bag corners. Attach "dream" wire word beneath butterfly with paper adhesive; let dry. Tie ribbon into a bow around handle; trim ends in V-notches. ∎

SOURCES: Corrugated paper, card and gift bag from DMD Inc.; wire from Toner Plastic Inc.; Zip Dry and Kid's Choice glue from Beacon; wire words from Making Memories.

MATERIALS

- 4 x 5¼-inch white gift bag
- 5 x 7-inch white card
- Tracing paper
- Dusty pink corrugated paper
- Pink and purple card stock
- Embroidery floss: variegated purple, variegated pink and olive green
- Black craft wire
- Mini butterfly punch
- Black fine-tip permanent marker
- Wire words: "dream" and "imagine"
- 17¼ inches ⅞-inch-wide ombre ribbon
- Sewing needle
- Instant-dry paper adhesive
- Instant-hold glue

Summer Tag

Design by DEANNA HUTCHISON

Torn and rolled paper gives a lifelike feel to the crashing waves; starfish and eyelets add dimension to this fun project.

Cut a 2¼ x 3¾-inch rectangle from light blue card stock; cut top two corners diagonally to form a tag shape. Use a computer or hand-print "Summer" onto vellum; cut a ½ x 2¾-inch rectangle around word and tear top and bottom edges. Apply blue chalk to torn edges and attach to center of tag with blue eyelets; trim ends.

Cut three 2¼ x 1¼-inch pieces of blue card stock; tear the top edge of each. Carefully roll the torn edges on two of the pieces. Layer and attach the rolled pieces to the bottom of the tag; trim edges. Apply double-sided tape to remaining blue strip; dip sticky side into sand and attach to bottom of tag. Use adhesive dots to attach the starfish embellishments. Punch a sun shape from yellow card stock and adhere above vellum.

Cut a small rectangle from blue card stock and position at top of tag; place a blue eyelet through rectangle and thread fibers through eyelet. ∎

SOURCES: Sun punch from Uchida of America.

MATERIALS

Card stock: light blue,
    blue and yellow
White vellum
Sun punch
Blue fibers
Blue chalk
Sand
3 small blue eyelets
2 starfish embellishments
Double-sided tape
Adhesive dots
Computer font (optional)

Book Tag

Design by MAUREEN SPELL

A real pocket from a worn pair of jeans becomes the base of a project that announces your love of books!

Cut a pocket off an old pair of blue jeans. Attach a "B" letter sticker onto olive green card stock; tear a rectangle around sticker and apply black ink to edges. Cut a 3 x 4-inch rectangle from purple card stock; tear rectangle in half to form a triangle that will fit onto library card. Apply embossing ink to edges of card stock and emboss with gold embossing powder. Place flower center on center of card stock.

Randomly emboss areas of the library card with gold embossing powder; adhere the embossed purple card stock to the bottom portion of the library card. Adhere the "B" rectangle toward top of library card and attach the letter stickers "ook" beside it. Use the label maker to type out the following quote except for "book": "A book is like a garden carried in the pocket." Attach words to card.

Adhere a piece of green fiber along the border of the purple card stock. Wrap several fibers around decorative brad and attach at top of tag. Use permanent double-sided tape to attach card to denim pocket. ■

SOURCES: Stickers from NRN Designs and Wordsworth; library card from Gaylord.

MATERIALS

Denim pocket
Olive green and purple
  card stock
Purple and green fibers
Flower sticker
Clear letter stickers
Library card
Embossing ink pad
Gold embossing powder
Heat embossing tool
Label maker
Decorative gold brad
Glue stick
Permanent double-sided
  tape

Into the Garden Book

Design by SUSAN STRINGFELLOW

Each page of this book is highlighted with fibers in colors that match the stunning photographs. If you don't have photos of your garden, use lifelike photo stickers instead.

Paint the front and back covers tan; let dry. Dry brush covers with ivory paint and rub some areas with brown, green and black ink. Repeat this process with the cork rectangle.

Stamp the letter "g" in the lower left corner of front cover with black acrylic paint; stamp the remaining words of the following sentiment with black solvent-based ink: "Into The Garden." Apply a coat of varnish to front and back covers.

Sponge paint the small flower cutout that came with the book kit with pink and ivory acrylic paint; let dry. Attach silk flowers to the cutout with a mini brad. Punch a small hole at the top and bottom of flower cutout; thread a piece of fiber through each hole and, referring to photo, tie to the top and bottom of the flower opening.

Stamp the tulip image and "flora" onto the cork rectangle; punch two holes in the bottom of the rectangle. Apply a coat of varnish; let dry. Cut several 3-inch lengths of green fibers; thread through holes and tie. Adhere cork piece in upper right corner of cover.

Continue to embellish each page of book with decorative papers, brads, fibers, flowers, etc. Once all pages are completed, stack them together along with front and back covers. Thread coil through holes to assemble book. ■

SOURCES: Book kit from The Little Scrapbook Store; tulip rubber stamp from Stampin' Up!; solvent-based ink pad from Tsukineko; foam stamp from Making Memories; alphabet rubber stamps from Rubber Stamp Ave.; cork rectangle from LazerLetterz.

MATERIALS

- Blank book kit with cutout flower opening
- Acrylic paint: pink, tan and ivory
- Brown and green ink pads
- Black solvent-based ink pad
- Large foam "g" stamp
- Small alphabet rubber stamps
- Tulip rubber stamp
- Assorted fibers
- Cork rectangle
- Varnish
- Assorted brads
- Silk flowers
- Assorted decorative papers
- Computer font (optional)
- Paintbrush
- Craft sponge
- Hole punch
- Craft glue
- Glue stick

Thank You Card

Design by SUSAN STRINGFELLOW

Wrap a stamped sentiment in soft boucle yarn to highlight the pretty flower image.

MATERIALS

White and peach
  card stock
Coordinating striped
  card stock
4 orange mini brads
Flower rubber stamp
Alphabet rubber stamps
Black solvent-based ink
  pad
Watermark ink pad
Acrylic paint: peach,
  pink and green
Paintbrush
Green fiber
Sanding block
Glue stick

Cut a 5½ x 8½-inch piece of white card stock; score and fold in half. Cut a 4 x 5¼-inch rectangle from peach card stock; sand edges and attach to card. Cut a 2¾ x 5½-inch strip of the striped card stock; sand the edges and attach toward the left side of card.

Use the watermark ink pad to stamp the flower image onto white card stock. Lightly paint flower; let dry. Stamp flower image on top of painted flower with the black solvent-based ink pad. Stamp "thank you" beside flower; cut a rectangle around image and adhere to card. Wrap green fiber around flower image and attach with orange mini brads; tie a bow in lower left corner. ∎

SOURCES: Mini brads from Making Memories; rubber stamps from Hero Arts; ink pads from Tsukineko.

Make A Wish

Design by JEANNE WYNHOFF

Send a little inspiration to a friend with this handsome pocket card. Ribbons and a shiny brad accent the top of the library card insert.

Apply gold leafing along edges of library pocket and card; let dry. Cut a piece of brown patterned paper to fit onto the pocket front; adhere. Cut a triangle from adhesive mesh and attach to pocket front; place a vintage sticker on top of mesh. Randomly place word stickers onto the inner and front sections of library pocket. Apply brown chalk to entire surface.

Punch a hole in library card; wrap fibers around gold brad and attach brad. Randomly place desired stickers on card and apply brown chalk over entire surface. Add splashes of metallic copper paint to both pieces. ■

SOURCES: Chalk from Craft-T Products; mesh from Magic Mesh; patterned paper from Provo Craft; vintage stickers from Karen Foster Design; clear word stickers from NRN Designs and The C-Thru Ruler Co./Deja Views; gold leafing pen from Krylon.

MATERIALS

Library pocket and card
Brown and natural fibers
Brown chalk
Adhesive brown mesh
Brown patterned paper
Coordinating vintage
    stickers
Clear word stickers
Gold leafing pen
Gold round brad
Metallic copper acrylic
    paint
Paintbrush
Sponge-tip applicator
Glue stick

Smile Tag Card

Design by SUSAN STRINGFELLOW

Lavish fiber tassels adorn the top of this unique card. Easy freehand vines are added with a marker and a trendy paint strip adds blocks of color.

MATERIALS

- Golden yellow card stock
- Brown textured vellum
- Pre-colored sunflower image
- Olive green paint strip
- "Smile" dimensional embellishment
- Cork square tag
- Green and yellow fibers
- Sanding block
- Sewing machine
- Brown sewing thread
- Vine border rubber stamp
- Green chalk-finish ink pad
- Brown ink pad
- Craft sponge
- Green square brad
- Hole punch
- Glue stick
- Craft glue

Cut a 5-inch square from golden yellow card stock; score and fold in half. With card closed, cut top corners diagonally to form a tag shape. Punch a hole at top. Apply brown ink to edges with craft sponge.

Use the green chalk-finish ink pad to stamp the vine image along the top and right edges of tag; stamp image inside tag along bottom and right edges. Cut a 4-inch piece from the paint strip; sand lightly and adhere to left side of tag.

With tag open, machine-sew along the left and bottom edges of tag using a zigzag stitch. Apply brown ink to edges of pre-colored sunflower image. Cut a 1 x 2-inch piece of brown textured vellum and adhere toward top right corner of tag; attach sunflower image on top of vellum. Attach cork square in bottom left corner; adhere "smile" embellishment on cork square.

Cut eight 8-inch lengths of fibers; thread four pieces through front tag hole and thread remaining fibers through back tag hole. ■

SOURCES: Pre-colored flower image, paint strip and sanding block from PM Designs; cork square tag from LazerLetterz; textured vellum from Golden Oaks; rubber stamp from Stampin' Up!; chalk-finish ink pad from Clearsnap; square brad from Accent Depot.

Tropical Escape

Design by SUSAN STRINGFELLOW

Next time you visit your favorite coffee shop, don't just toss away the cup wrapper and coffee fact card. Add a cupcake topper and recycle everything into a fun tag!

Cut tropical coffee ad into a 2¾ x 5-inch rectangle. Cut a 2 x 3-inch piece from corrugated cardboard; tear the top edge and attach to bottom half of coffee ad. Use alphabet stamps and brown ink to stamp "ESCAPE!" onto off-white card stock; sponge blue chalk-finish ink over stamped letters. Cut a rectangle around words and attach toward top of coffee ad; frame word with cork book plate. Punch holes through book plate holes; thread fibers through and knot.

Adhere dimensional tiki man embellishment to corrugated cardboard. Wrap four 4-inch pieces of fiber around bottom of tag; secure ends in back. Attach silk flowers around bottom portion using mini brads. ■

SOURCES: Cork book plate from LazerLetterz; mini brads from Making Memories; alphabet rubber stamps from Rubber Stamp Ave.; ink pads from Tsukineko and Clearsnap.

MATERIALS

- Tropical coffee ad flyer
- Corrugated cardboard
- Off-white card stock
- Cork book plate
- Coordinating fibers
- Tiki man dimensional embellishment
- Silk flowers
- Mini brads
- Alphabet rubber stamps
- Brown solvent-based ink pad
- Blue chalk-finish ink pad
- Craft sponge
- Hole punch
- Craft glue

MATERIALS

Tag book kit (includes 12
  tags, fibers and a 4-
  inch wire coil)
Several journey-themed
  quotes
Round metal letters
Word rub-on transfers
Word stickers
Assorted patterned papers
Assorted stickers
Various decorative metal
  brads and eyelets
Various embellishments
  such as charms, clips,
  silk flowers, etc.
Fibers
Silver cord
Assorted chalk-finish ink
  pads
Label maker with label
  tape
Hole punch
Adhesive foam squares
Permanent adhesive dots
Industrial-strength glue
Computer font (optional)

Joy in the Journey Tag Book

Design by JANE SWANSON

Filled with inspirational quotes about journeys near and far, this tag book serves as a wonderful gift to someone whose journey is just beginning!

Adhere patterned paper to front cover; trim edges even with adhesive dots. Cut two more various size pieces of different patterned papers; apply black ink to edges. Punch holes along top edge of one piece; adhere pieces to front cover and trim edges if needed. Transfer desired word onto cover; adhere metal letters with industrial-strength glue. Use a computer or hand-print desired title of book; cut a rectangle around title and apply black ink to edges. Adhere to cover.

Choose several journey-themed quotes and use label maker, word stickers, metal letters, etc. to form quotes onto tags. Adhere various papers to each tag and embellish with charms, stickers, eyelets, etc. Add

black ink to the edges of each tag and to the back and front cover edges. When tags are finished, align the tags and gently thread the wire coil through the holes. Cut a piece of silver cord and wrap around book; tie a knot to keep book shut. ∎

SOURCES: Tag book kit from The Little Scrapbook Store; round metal letters, brads and rub-on word transfers from Making Memories; stickers from Pebbles Inc. and Sassafras Lass; chalk-finish ink pads from Clearsnap.

Happy Birthday

Design by JEANNE WYNHOFF

Sometimes less is more, as illustrated by the very effective single strand of blue fiber adorning this masculine card.

MATERIALS

Blue fiber

Tan and dark blue card
    stock

Brown chalk

Craft sponge

Fishing lures images

Transparency sheet

Craft stick

Black fine-tip permanent
    marker

Mini square punch

Adhesive dots

Computer font (optional)

Score and fold an 8½ x 11-inch sheet of tan card stock in half. Cut a 4½ x 5½-inch piece of blue card stock; tear one of the short edges and adhere toward top of card.

Punch out twelve squares from blue card stock; set aside. Cut four 2 x 2¼-inch rectangles of tan card stock and adhere to card referring to photo for placement. Add detail lines with black fine-tip marker and apply brown chalk to entire surface of card. Attach a fishing lure image to each tan rectangle.

Use a computer to print "Happy Birthday" onto transparency.

Note: Print message in reverse — so when it is transferred, it will be correct. Use craft stick to rub message onto card.

Option: Use black marker to hand-write message onto transparency. Attach blue squares to card and adhere a piece of blue fiber along torn edge of blue card stock. ❧

SOURCES: Fishing images and mini square punch from EK Success; chalk from Craf-T Products.

Library Pocket Card

Design by JEANNE WYNHOFF

Create one of these fun cards for each member of your family. Every so often, add a handwtitten sentiment to remind them of your love!"

Attach two decorative border stickers to the bottom edge of the library pocket; trim edges. Cut a triangle from adhesive mesh and attach to lower left corner. Cut a 2⅜ x 3½-inch rectangle from mesh; attach to top inside portion of pocket. Trim edges even with pocket.

Place desired stickers randomly onto the top mesh section; add button, key and alphabet stickers to bottom front pocket. Apply brown chalk over entire surface. Use adhesive dots to attach the cork filmstrip piece to desired photo; attach to pocket.

Trim the top edges of library card diagonally; punch a hole at top and loop fibers through. Attach desired stickers to card; add stitch marks with black fine-tip marker and apply brown chalk to entire surface. Randomly add splashes of metallic copper paint to both surfaces. ∎

SOURCES: Cork filmstrip from LazerLetterz; chalk from Craf-T Products; mesh from Magic Mesh; stickers from Karen Foster Design and alphabet stickers from EK Success.

MATERIALS

Library pocket and card
Brown fibers
Cork filmstrip shape
Brown chalk
Sponge-tip applicator
Adhesive brown mesh
Vintage alphabet stickers
Leaf, key, button and
    decorative border stickers
Black fine-tip marker
Metallic copper acrylic paint
Small photo
Adhesive dots
Paintbrush

Merci Card

Design by JEANNE WYNHOFF

Present your thanks to a special someone with European style. Scans of an antique postcard and postage add a decidedly vintage touch!

MATERIALS

Navy blue and brown
   card stock
Tan patterned paper
Cream mesh
Coordinating fibers
Transparency sheets
French postcard image
Old postage stamp images
Sticker making machine
Black marker
Metallic rub-on cream
Makeup sponge
2 mini round brads
Tag punch
Small piece of
   cross-stitch fabric
Adhesive dots
Repositionable adhesive
Computer and scanner

Cut a 5½ x 8½-inch piece of navy blue card stock; score and fold in half. Cut a piece of tan patterned paper 4¼ x 5½ inches; cut piece diagonally leaving one side larger than the other. Adhere to card lining up bottom and left edges. Cut a similar sized piece of mesh and adhere on top of tan piece using adhesive dots in the corners.

Use a computer and scanner to print old postage stamp images onto a transparency sheet; cut out a 5¼ x 2½-inch rectangle around images and attach to the mesh with adhesive dots. Insert brads in the bottom corners of card; wrap a piece of fiber around one of the brads and run it across card to wrap around the remaining brad.

Print a French postcard image onto a transparency sheet; cut out image and run it through the sticker making machine. Attach to a piece of brown card stock; trim edges and adhere to card.

Attach cross-stitch fabric to a sheet of card stock ½ inch from top with repositionable adhesive. Use a computer to print "merci" onto fabric; cut a 1¼ x ¾-inch rectangle around word and pull out a few strands of fabric. Remove card stock from back of word; use makeup sponge and metallic rub-on cream to add color to edges of word. Punch a tag shape from brown card stock; outline with black marker. Attach word rectangle to tag; punch a hole and loop fibers through. Attach tag to card. ■

SOURCES: Patterned paper from Provo Craft; metallic rub-on cream from Craf-T Products; tag punch from EK Success

For My Special Valentine

Design by JEANNE WYNHOFF

Simple cross-stitches in the corners anchor printed paper to the front of a valentine fit for the special man in your life!

MATERIALS

- Brown and tan card stock
- Red patterned paper
- Thin brown fibers
- Hearts and tags card stock stickers
- Brown chalk
- Gold round brad
- Sewing needle
- Black fine-tip marker
- Glue stick
- Computer font (optional)

Score and fold an 8½ x 11-inch sheet of brown card stock in half. Cut a 4⅞ x 7¾-inch piece of red patterned paper; adhere to card. Use sewing needle and thin brown fibers to stitch an "x" in each corner.

Attach large heart sticker to tan card stock; tear edges and add border detail with black fine-tip marker. Apply brown chalk to torn edges. Use a mini brad to attach a small tag sticker to heart. Adhere piece to left side of card.

Tear the bottom edge of a large tag sticker; apply brown chalk to edge. Adhere a torn piece of tan card stock to tag; add detail lines with black marker. Apply brown chalk and continue to embellish with desired stickers. Loop fibers through hole in tag and adhere assembled piece to card.

Use a computer or hand-print "For my special Valentine" onto tan card stock; apply brown chalk to edges and adhere to card. Print out letters for desired name onto tan card stock; cut letters into squares. Apply chalk to edges and attach to card.

If desired, use a computer or hand-print a message onto tan card stock; cut around message and adhere inside card. Add heart stickers and brown chalk to edges. ■

SOURCES: Card stock stickers from Pebbles Inc.; chalk from Craf-T Products; mini brad from Making Memories.

Smile, Love, Adore Frame

Design by SAHILY GONZALEZ

Create a dozen of these frames for all your teen's friends— they're easy to make and they're great locker decorations!

Brushing unevenly, paint the frame mat with red and pink acrylic paints; let dry. Attach assorted word and definition stickers around frame; attach alphabet stickers to spell out names or initials. Apply inks to edges of stickers as desired; attach flower stickers. Wrap fiber ends around brads and attach to top of frame to form a hanger. Apply a coat of decoupage medium to entire surface; let dry. Attach photo to backside of frame. ∎

SOURCES: Stickers from Making Memories, EK Success and NRN Designs; solvent-based black ink pad from Tsukineko.

MATERIALS

White frame mat
Red fibers
Assorted word and
    definition stickers
Alphabet stickers
Assorted flower stickers
Pink and red acrylic paint
2 silver brads
Black solvent-based ink
    pad
Brown ink pad
Decoupage medium
Paintbrush

Journey & Adventure

Design by JEANNE WYNHOFF

Tuck a little mad money in the pocket of this journey card to wish your traveling friend well!

MATERIALS

Blue fibers
Dark blue and light blue
    card stock
Blue chalk
2 large silver round brads
Small silver round brad
Silver metal mesh
"Adventure" and
    "Journey" rubber
    stamps
Black ink pad
Blue splattered mesh
Watch face, watch hand
    and ship images
Twill tape
2 small washers
Aluminum sheet
1½- and ½-inch square
    punches
Adhesive dots
Wire cutters

For tag pocket, cut a piece of dark blue card stock 3 x 3⅞ inches; score and fold ¼ inch in on the two long sides. Cut another piece of dark blue card stock 2½ x 4¼ inches; round the two bottom corners. Score the round bottom edge and fold upward. Turn rounded piece over and insert it into the other piece; wrap rounded section around bottom toward front of pocket and attach with adhesive dots. Fold the two side edges over and adhere. Referring to photo, cut a small rounded half oval into top layer of pocket.

Attach a 2½ x 2¼-inch piece of blue splattered mesh to front of pocket; trim edges even. Punch a 1½-inch square from the metal mesh. Insert a brad through a washer and metal mesh square; trim the prongs with wire cutters and attach with adhesive dots to pocket.

Adhere watch hand to watch face image and attach to metal mesh on pocket. Wrap fibers around pocket and secure with adhesive dots in the back. Stamp "Journey" in the upper left corner.

For tag, cut a 2 x 4-inch rectangle from light blue card stock; cut top two corners diagonally to form a tag shape. Punch a hole at top and loop fibers through. Attach a 2 x 2¼-inch piece of blue splattered mesh to tag; trim edges even.

Punch a 1½-inch square from metal mesh. Punch a ½-inch square from aluminum sheet; place a small silver brad through aluminum and adhere to metal mesh. Insert a brad through a washer and through metal mesh; attach assembled metal piece to tag by inserting brad through tag.

Cut out ship image; crumple up and carefully smooth out. Apply blue chalk and attach to tag. Apply blue chalk to exposed areas of the tag; cut a 2½-inch piece of twill tape and apply blue chalk to entire surface. Stamp "adventure" onto twill tape; adhere to tag securing ends in back. Insert tag into pocket. ∎

SOURCES: Chalks from Craf-T Products; brads and metal mesh from Making Memories; watch face and ship images from Hot Off The Press; watch hand image and 1/2-inch square punch from EK Success.

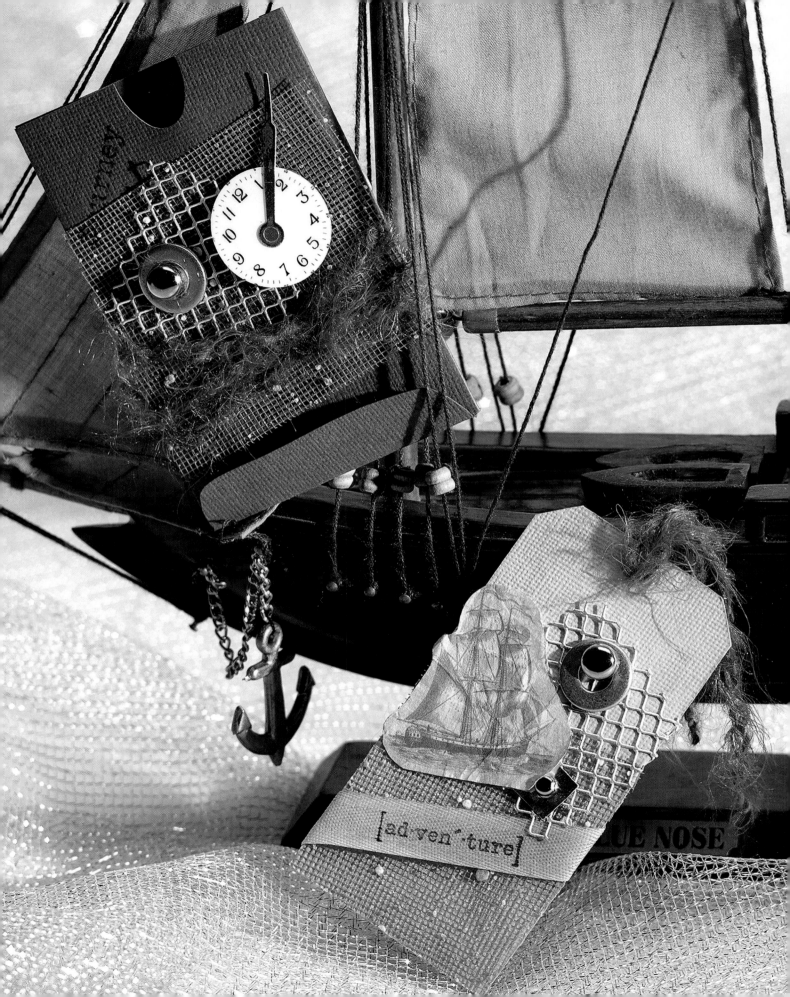

[ad·ven´ture]

BLUE NOSE

Seashell Card

Design by LARA GUSTAFSON

Softly spun thick and thin fiber mimics the torn paper accents on this striking greeting card.

MATERIALS

Card stock: light blue,
      dark blue and brown
Ivory textured paper
Green fibers
3 seashell images
2 blue eyelets
Blue ink pad
Walnut ink
Sandpaper
Double-sided tape

Score and fold an 8½ x 11-inch sheet of light blue card stock in half. Cut three seashell images into 1¾-inch squares; mount each image onto brown card stock with double-sided tape. Trim card stock into 2¼-inch squares.

Apply walnut ink to ivory textured paper. Once dry, sand lightly. Tear one long edge of textured paper creating a strip approximately 1¾ inch wide; apply blue ink to torn edge and attach to left side of card with two eyelets. Thread fibers through eyelets securing ends inside with tape.

Mount seashell images to card front; tear ¼ inch off from right edge of card. Attach a 5½ x 8½-inch piece of dark blue card stock inside card covering up fiber ends. ∎

SOURCES: Textured paper from Club Scrap Inc.; seashell images from Altered Pages; eyelets from Making Memories.

Happy Independence Day

Design by JEANNE WYNHOFF

Red, white and blue acrylic paints add patriotic flair to this greeting card!

Cut a 5½ x 8½-inch piece of red card stock; score and fold in half. Cut a 2 x 4¼-inch piece of white mesh; pull out a few strands to create fraying. Apply adhesive to mesh with adhesive cartridge and applicator and attach to center of card front. Use an adhesive eraser to remove excess adhesive.

Cut a 4¼ x 1⅞-inch piece of blue card stock; adhere to right side of card. Apply white paint to the edges of card with foam brush; let dry. Use the star dies to cut out two large stars and five small stars from cork paper. Apply red, white and blue stripes to the large stars; paint the small stars red, white and blue individually. Let each dry completely.

Stamp "Happy 4th of July" onto left side of card. Twist fibers together and tie into a bow; adhere in upper right corner. Attach cork stars with adhesive dots. ∎

SOURCES: Cork sheet from LazerLetterz; rubber stamps from Stampendous and The Artful Lexicon; Sizzix star dies and die cutter from Ellison; adhesive cartridge and applicator from Xyron.

MATERIALS
Cork paper
Red, white and blue fibers
Red and blue card stock
White mesh
Acrylic paint: red, white and blue
3 foam brushes
Assorted "Happy 4th of July" rubber stamps
Dark blue ink pad
Small and large star dies and die cutter
Adhesive dots
Adhesive eraser
Adhesive cartridge and applicatpr

Giggles Tag

Design by SUSAN HUBER

For the young, or young-at-heart—this reminder to smile at every opportunity!

MATERIALS

Pink card stock
Pink vellum
Green swirled vellum
Coordinating fibers
Metal-edge flower tag
Coordinating
  dimensional stickers
Blue mini brad
Hole punch

Cut pink card stock 2½ x 4 inches; cut two top corners diagonally to form a tag shape. Cut green swirled vellum into a tag shape slightly smaller than pink tag; repeat with pink vellum. Layer tags together; place metal-edge flower tag at top of layers and punch a hole at top. Attach a brad through hole to hold layers together.

Wind fibers around brad; trim ends. Place dimensional stickers on flower tag and toward bottom of pink vellum. ■

SOURCES: Vellum and dimensional stickers from EK Success; metal-edge flower tag from Making Memories.

Coffee Addict Altered Tin

Design by MAUREEN SPELL

Recycle that CD tin you just received and turn it into a gift for a java-loving friend. Tuck a tiny magnet inside for a doubly-good surprise!

Sand the top and bottom of tin with sandpaper; adhere decorative paper to the front, back and inside lid. *Note: Do not cover the bottom sides with paper because the tin will be difficult to close.* Cut out various coffee-themed images and adhere them to tin. Apply dimensional adhesive over some of the images; let dry.

Cut three 2½-inch pieces of brown fibers; adhere them to tin in a wavy pattern to represent coffee steam. Use alphabet stickers to spell out "ADDICT"; ink the edges of each sticker and place onto tin beneath fibers. Apply dimensional adhesive on top of stickers. Glue heart clip onto tin.

Paint edges of tin with brown acrylic paint. Rub clear embossing ink onto corners; emboss with gold embossing powder. Apply black solvent-based ink to bottom edges.

Use a computer or hand-print different coffee sayings onto white card stock; ink edges with brown ink. Adhere inside lid. ∎

SOURCES: Decorative paper from Rusty Pickle; coffee images from Altered Pages; heart clip from Making Memories; alphabet stickers from EK Success; Diamond Glaze adhesive from JudiKins.

MATERIALS

- Metal tin
- Brown decorative paper
- Brown acrylic paint
- Brown ink pad
- Clear embossing ink pad
- Gold embossing powder
- Black solvent-based ink pad
- Coffee-themed images
- Brown fibers
- Heart metal clip
- Alphabet stickers
- Walnut ink
- Sandpaper
- Clear dimensional adhesive
- Embossing heat tool
- Paintbrush
- Computer (optional)

Fall Fibers Place Card

Design by LAURIE D'AMBROSIO

MATERIALS

- 3½ x 4-inch ivory card stock
- Gold mulberry paper
- Gray-green textured paper
- Leaf sticker
- Alphabet rubber stamps
- Black solvent-based ink pad
- Watermark ink pad
- Copper opalescent pigment powder
- Copper fibers
- Rectangle punch
- Adhesive dots
- Plastic wrap
- Paintbrush

Rust-colored eyelash yarn adds an autumn touch to this place card. For a unique dinner party favor, personalize the inside with a sentiment just for the person whose name appears on the front!

Fold card stock in half; cut the two corners on the left side diagonally to form a tag shape. Trace tag shape onto gold mulberry paper with a wet paintbrush; tear out shape and adhere to place card. Punch a rectangle at left side of tag through top layer only.

Use alphabet rubber stamps to stamp desired name onto gray-green paper with black ink; tear around name and attach to place card. Add a leaf sticker to card. Crumple up a piece of plastic wrap and use it to apply ink from the watermark ink pad to the place card. With a dry paintbrush, dust the ink with a small amount of copper pigment powder. Cut two 6-inch pieces of fiber; loop through hole. ∎

SOURCES: Mulberry paper and textured paper from Black Ink; leaf sticker from Die Cuts with a View; alphabet rubber stamps from Plaid/All Night Media; ink pads from Tsukineko; pigment powder from Jacquard Products.

Autumn Foliage CD

Design by SAM COUSINS

Instead of creating a tassel, wrap fiber around an altered CD for a unique look!

Randomly paint entire surface of CD with pink, orange and yellow acrylic paints; let dry completely. Trace the CD onto patterned paper; cut out and tear paper into pieces. Adhere a few torn pieces to CD allowing acrylic paint to be seen. Apply silver leafing to edges of CD; outline silver leafing with black fine-tip pen.

Tear edges of photo; lightly brush orange paint to torn edges and attach photo to CD. Create autumn-themed words using label maker. Embellish patterned paper blocks with label words and rub-on transfers. Adhere blocks to CD. Weave orange and yellow fibers around and through CD; secure ends in back with tape. Add pink fiber around edge; attach magnets to back. ∎

SOURCES: Patterned papers and paper blocks from KI Memories; silver leafing pen from Krylon; rub-on transfers from Making Memories.

MATERIALS

Blank compact disc
Acrylic paint: pink, orange and yellow
Pink and orange patterned paper
Pink and orange patterned paper blocks
Fibers: pink, orange and yellow
Silver leafing pen
Black fine-tip pen
Word rub-on transfers
Label maker with label tape
Autumn-themed photo
Magnets
Glue stick
Craft glue
Tape
Paintbrush

Military Journal

Design by JEANNE WYNHOFF

Create a one-of-a-kind, handmade journal for your favorite military personnel. Metallic paper and a beaded chain resemble dog tags!

Cut 15 sheets of white card stock 10 x $7\frac{11}{16}$ inches; score each down the middle and fold in half. Attach each sheet back to back with double-sided tape, leaving the first and back pages without adhesive.

Cut two $7\frac{7}{8}$ x $5\frac{1}{8}$-inch pieces of cardboard. Lay a 9 x 12-inch piece of military-themed patterned paper face down on work surface; miter-cut the corners. Score each side of patterned paper $\frac{1}{2}$ inch from edge and fold; crease with a bone folder. Place one cardboard piece on each end of patterned paper; adhere and fold the scored edges over. Attach with double-sided tape. The gap in the middle between the cardboard pieces allows room for the card stock sheets inside journal.

Cut a 20-inch piece of fiber; center it across the inside cover and attach with adhesive dots. Attach the first page of the white folded card stock to the inside front cover; attach last card stock page to the inside back cover. ***Note:*** *Do not leave journal open when completing this step.* Covers need to be folded together to create a clean binding.

Place assorted stickers on front; sand lightly. Use a computer to print desired name or message onto metallic paper; emboss with silver embossing powder. Cut a dog tag shape around words; cut another blank dog tag. Layer tags and punch a hole through both; thread ball chain through holes and attach to front cover. Use adhesive dots to hold ball chain in place. ∎

SOURCES: Patterned paper from Frances Meyer; stickers from Karen Foster Design.

MATERIALS

Green fibers
Military-themed paper
Silver metallic paper
White card stock
Cardboard
Small piece of ball chain
Silver embossing powder
Heat embossing tool
Military-themed stickers
Bone folder
Sandpaper
Double-sided tape
Adhesive dots
Computer font

Winter Memories CD

Design by JEANNE WYNHOFF

Wintry paper embellished with stamped, embossed snowflakes forms the background for a favorite photo surrounded by a slide frame.

MATERIALS

Light blue patterned
    papers
Blank compact disc
White and blue fibers
"Memories" rub-on
    transfer
2 small white snowflake
    embellishments
Slide mount
White ink pad
Clear embossing powder
Heat embossing tool
Snowflake rubber stamp
Adhesive dots
Hole punch
Craft knife
Small photo

Punch a hole through top of CD. Tear a few pieces of assorted patterned papers; adhere pieces to CD overlapping edges. Trim excess paper so edges are even. Randomly stamp snowflake image onto CD; emboss with clear embossing powder.

Cover slide mount with patterned paper; cut out center with a craft knife and trim edges. Apply "memories" to bottom of slide mount; attach photo and adhere to CD.

Wrap fibers around CD and secure in back; thread fibers through hole and tie. Attach snowflake embellishments; cover the back of CD with paper and trim edges even. ∎

SOURCES: Patterned papers from Frances Meyer; rub-on transfer from Making Memories; rubber stamps from Hero Arts.

Sun-sational Wishes

Design by KATHLEEN PANEITZ

Send sunny birthday greetings to a special friend with this quick and easy card.

Cut burnt orange card stock 6 x 10 inches; score and fold in half. Moisten a paper towel with bleach and apply bleach to sun image with paper towel; stamp onto card front. ***Note:*** *Practice this technique before stamping onto card.* Do not get stamp overly wet with bleach and clean stamp thoroughly after using since bleach is corrosive. Allow image to turn white, which may take a few minutes.

Cut a piece of twill tape and adhere across bottom of card; use alphabet rubber stamps and black ink pad to stamp "wishes" onto tape. Secure tape with mini brads.

Cut a 2¼ x 4¾-inch rectangle from yellow daisy patterned paper; tear one long edge and adhere to left side of card overlapping twill tape. Use a computer or hand-print 'Sun'sational Birthday onto cream card stock; cut rectangles around both words. Apply brown chalk to edges and adhere words overlapping onto upper left corner of card.

Tie a double strand of natural raffia through and around top of card. Form a flower shape from yellow paper wire; secure flower to card with silver concho. ∎

SOURCES: Patterned paper from Colorbök; foam stamp and rubber stamps from Duncan/PSX; paper wire from Paperabilities; silver concho from Scrapworks; chalk from Craf-T Products; mini brads from Magic Scraps.

MATERIALS

- Burnt orange and cream card stock
- Yellow daisy patterned paper
- Sun foam stamp
- Bleach
- Paper towels
- Yellow paper wire
- Round silver concho
- Twill tape
- Alphabet rubber stamps
- Black ink pad
- Brown chalk
- 3 mini brads
- Natural raffia
- Glue stick
- Computer font (optional)

Home Is Love

Design by SAHILY GONZALEZ

Cover house-shaped cardboard with rubber-stamped papers and bind with cord to create a wonderful journal of building your first home.

Use a craft knife to cut a house shape from cardboard. *Note: An easy way to do this is to first cut a square of any size and then cut the top two corners diagonally to form a triangle-shaped top.* Cut another house from cardboard the same size as first; cut second one in half vertically forming the front cover which will open up to reveal the pages. Adhere red and off-white patterned card stock to the front and back of both cardboard pieces.

Use ivory acrylic paint to stamp desired last name at top of front cover. *Note: Divide name in half and stamp half on left side of cover and half on right side.* Adhere a 3½-inch-wide strip of home sentiment patterned paper across the middle of front cover; trim ends. Stamp decorative border around the edges of the front cover with brown acrylic paint.

Cut a rectangle from architectural patterned paper that resembles the shape of a door; adhere to a piece of card stock cut the same size to add strength. Center door on front cover and glue half of the door to right side of cover.

Adhere a photo to left side of front cover; cut an architectural image and adhere next to door. Use a computer to print out the word "love" and desired initials. *Note: Alphabet circle tags may be substituted in place of computer font.* Cut out circles around letters; adhere "love" vertically overlapping architectural image. Adhere initials underneath photo and stamp an ampersand between initials.

Attach a brad on left edge of door; use craft glue to adhere key embellishment on top of brad allowing brad to show through key. Use alphabet stickers to spell out "Home" on top of door; use label maker to make rest of quote: "is where the heart is." Cut words apart and attach "is" underneath "Home" and attach rest of quote on the left side inside front cover.

For inside pages, cut off-white card stock into the same shape as covers. Punch three holes on the left side on half of the pages; punch three holes on the right side on the remaining pages. Line up pages with covers and punch cover holes on left and right sides; tie pages together with hemp cord. Decorate inside pages as desired. ■

SOURCES: Patterned papers from 7 Gypsies, Creative Imaginations and Doodlebug Design; key embellishment from Li'l Davis; foam stamps from Making Memories; stickers from Cloud 9 Designs.

MATERIALS

Cardboard
Card stock: red, off-white and gold patterned
Architectural and home sentiment patterned papers
Key embellishment
Small brad
Hemp cord
Alphabet and decorative border foam stamps
Ivory and brown acrylic paint
Alphabet stickers
Alphabet circle tags (optional)
Label maker with label tape
Sponge brush
Craft knife
Glue stick
Craft glue
Computer font (optional)

Vintage Memories

Design by KATHY WEGNER

Fibers and buttons combine with vintage-look papers to create a card ideal for any occasion.

MATERIALS

- 5⅛ x 7-inch blank ivory card with envelope
- Black/ivory patterned paper
- 3 (2¾ x 4¼-inch) postcard images
- Beige eyelash fiber
- 3 beige buttons
- White thread
- Jute
- Sewing needle
- Decorative-edge scissors
- Adhesive dots
- Double-sided tape

Use decorative-edge scissors to cut black/ivory patterned paper 4½ x 6¼ inches; apply double-sided tape around the perimeter on the backside of patterned paper. Attach eyelash fibers to double-sided tape; adhere paper to card. Overlap three postcard images joining them together with adhesive dots; tie jute around postcards and tie a bow in front. Adhere postcards to card. Sew thread through buttons; attach buttons to card with adhesive dots.

SOURCES: Patterned paper from Anna Griffin Inc.

Gone Fishing Birthday Wishes

Design by JEANNE WYNHOFF

Your favorite fisherman will receive the wishes he's beenfishin' for when you give him this special card crafted just for him!

Cut a 5½ x 8½-inch piece of dark green card stock; score and fold in half. Cut a 5 x 3⅞-inch piece of patterned paper; punch a hole in each corner and attach green rivets. Use adhesive dots to attach scrap of burlap in lower right corner. Cut a 5½-inch piece of fiber and thread it through cork slide buckle. Position fiber on bottom of patterned paper wrapping ends around to back and securing with adhesive dots. Attach assembled piece to card.

Remove shanks from buttons and adhere to burlap piece; use sponge-tip applicator to apply metallic green rub-on cream around edges of patterned paper, onto burlap piece, buttons and cork buckle. Use a computer to print "Happy Birthday" onto a transparency sheet. *Option: Use a permanent marker to write sentiment by hand. Note: Print words in reverse so they will appear in the correct direction when transferred to card.* Rub printed transparency onto card with a bone folder or craft stick. ∎

SOURCES: Patterned paper from K&Company; cork slide buckle from LazerLetterz; metallic rub-on cream from Craf-T Products; fishing-themed buttons from Jesse James & Co.

MATERIALS

Green and natural fibers
Dark green card stock
Fishing patterned paper
Transparency sheet
Small cork slide buckle
2 fishing-themed buttons
Metallic green
    rub-on cream
Scrap of burlap
4 green rivets
Black fine-tip
    permanent marker
Sponge-tip applicator
Button shank remover
Bone folder or craft stick
Hole punch
Adhesive dots
Computer font (optional)

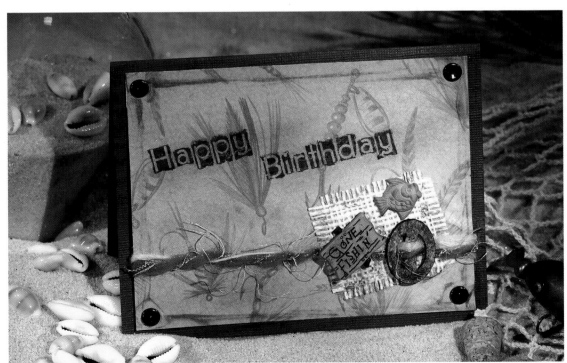

Explore Accordion Tag Card

Design by JEANNE WYNHOFF

Attach photos and other souvenirs to the tags tucked inside this card to remind you of a special weekend adventure.

MATERIALS

Brown fibers

12 x 12-inch light brown card stock

Brown crackle patterned paper

Coordinating stickers and art images

Black ink pad

Black and brown chalk

Alphabet brass stencils

Oval punch

Hole punch

Stamping sponge

Craft stick or bone folder

Adhesive dots

Glue stick

Fold a 12 x 12-inch sheet of light brown card stock in half; accordion fold into four vertical pockets. Crease each fold with a craft stick or bone folder. Cut a 12 x 5¾-inch strip of patterned paper; tear top edge and loosely adhere it across the outside of accordion pocket. Refold pocket accordion-style with patterned paper attached; make adjustments as needed and completely adhere paper.

Tear the first pocket horizontally halfway down; for second pocket, cut 1 inch down from top straight across and use oval punch to punch an oval sideways at top of pocket. On the third pocket, cut straight across 2¼ inches down; cut down the sides 1¼ inches and fold down the card stock. For last pocket, tear diagonally starting approximately 1¼ inches from top. Secure side pocket edges with glue to keep pockets closed.

Use craft sponge and alphabet brass stencils to rub "EXPLORE" across pocket fronts. Apply black and brown chalk to entire surface; apply extra on edges. Add desired stickers and art images to front and back.

Cut four 2½ x 5-inch rectangles from crackle patterned paper; cut top two corners in each to form tags. Punch holes and loop fibers through. Apply black chalk to tag edges. Insert tags into pockets; tie shut with fiber. ∎

SOURCES: Patterned paper from Provo Craft; chalk from Craf-T Products; stickers from Karen Foster Design; paper art images from Hot Off The Press.

Autumn Tag

Design by DEANNA HUTCHISON

The unique little pumpkin on the front of this tag is created from artfully torn paper!

MATERIALS

Dark orange and dark
   green card stock
Patterned papers: light
   orange, dark orange
   and orange plaid
2 copper brads
Orange and green fibers
Dark green paper wire
Black fine-tip marker
Paper crimper
Hole punch
Adhesive foam tape
Glue stick
Computer font (optional)

Cut orange plaid paper 2¼ x 3¾ inches; cut top two corners to create a tag shape. Cut a 3½ x ½-inch strip of dark green card stock; run strip through paper crimper. Use a computer or hand-print "Autumn" onto a ⅜ x 3½-inch strip of dark orange card stock leaving room for a brad on each side. Run strip through paper crimper and trim so it fits onto dark green strip; layer strips on top of each other and attach at an angle to orange plaid tag with copper brads. Trim ends if needed.

Adhere orange plaid tag to a 2½ x 4-inch piece of dark orange card stock; cut top two corners off. Glue cut-off corners to bottom portion of orange plaid portion.

Referring to photo, tear a circle from dark orange patterned paper; tear a smaller circle from light orange patterned paper and glue to dark orange circle to form a pumpkin. Tear two small strips of dark orange patterned paper; adhere to layered circles. Tear a small piece of dark green card stock for pumpkin stem; glue behind pumpkin.

Cut a 3½-inch piece of dark green paper wire and fold in half; curl ends and attach to back of pumpkin. Attach pumpkin to tag with adhesive foam tape. Cut a small square from dark orange card stock; glue at top of tag and punch a hole through it. Thread fiber ends through hole and back through formed loop. ∎

SOURCES: Patterned papers from Keeping Memories Alive.

Thanksgiving Tag

Design by SUSAN STRINGFELLOW

Embellish a dimensional stamped tag with fibers in all the brilliant colors of autumn!

Cut a 3½ x 4½-inch piece of brown card stock; tear the bottom edge. Dampen piece with water and crumple up; allow to dry. Gently uncrumple paper and rub brown ink across entire surface and on edges. Stamp vine and swirl images across bottom of crumpled piece using burgundy and dark green ink. Punch a hole and attach large gold eyelet at top forming a tag.

Stamp pumpkin and fall images such as acorns, leaves and vegetables onto a piece of light gold card stock with assorted ink colors; cut out motif and tear the top edge. Rub motif and edges with tan chalk-finish ink. Punch a hole in the upper left and lower right corners; cut three 6-inch lengths of fibers and thread them through holes. Attach piece to crumpled tag.

Cut a 1 x 3-inch piece of natural mesh; attach to upper right corner of tag. Cut six 6-inch lengths of fibers; loop fibers through eyelet. Stamp "Happy Thanksgiving" onto patterned paper using tan chalk-finish ink pad; cut a rectangle around words and tear side edges. Mat onto dark brown card stock and tear side edges. Apply golden yellow and brown ink randomly to surface. Attach toward top of tag with adhesive foam tape. ∎

SOURCES: "Happy Thanksgiving" rubber stamp from Close To My Heart; rubber stamps and ink pads from Stampin' Up!; Chalk-finish ink pad from Creative Beginnings; Mesh from Altered Pages.

MATERIALS

Card stock: brown, dark brown and light gold
Coordinating patterned paper
Fall colored fibers
Rubber stamps: "Happy Thanksgiving," pumpkin, vine, swirl, acorns, leaves and vegetables
Ink pads: burgundy, dark green, orange, golden yellow and brown
Tan chalk-finish ink pad
Large gold eyelet
Natural mesh
Glue stick
Hole punch

Country Christmas Tag

Design by DEANNA HUTCHISON

Raffia and paper punches make creating this gift tag a snap. Torn papers give this project a real country feel.

MATERIALS

Tan and red card stock
Red plaid patterned paper
Tree and heart punches
Natural raffia
Gold embroidery floss
Adhesive foam dots
Hole punch
Glue stick

Cut tan card stock 2¾ x 4½ inches; trim top two corners into a rounded tag shape. Cut a slightly smaller rounded tag shape from red plaid patterned paper; adhere to tan tag. Tear a 4½ x 1½-inch strip from tan card stock; adhere to center of tag. Tear a 4½ x 1¼-inch strip from red card stock; adhere on top of tan strip.

Punch two trees and one heart from tan card stock. Lay a 5-inch piece of gold embroidery floss on torn red strip. Attach punched trees and heart on top of embroidery floss with adhesive foam dots to hold the floss in place. Punch hole at end of tag. Cut a piece of raffia and fold in half; insert raffia ends through hole and back through formed loop. Pull taut.

SOURCES: Tree and heart punches from EK Success.

Sparkle Christmas Tag

Design by DEANNA HUTCHISON

Add just the right amount of sparkle to this simple gift tag with a few lines of glitter paint.

Cut a 2½ x 4½-inch rectangle from red card stock; cut top two corners to form a tag shape. Cut a 2¼ x 3-inch piece of glittered patterned paper and tear in half diagonally. Tear off more on one torn edge to create a gap in the middle. Referring to photo, adhere torn pieces to tag leaving gap in the center.

Use a computer or hand-print "Merry Christmas!" onto red card stock; cut a ⅝ x 3⅛-inch rectangle around words. Attach rectangle to tag with gold brads. Punch hole at top of tag and thread green raffia through. ■

SOURCES: Patterned paper from K&Company.

MATERIALS
Red card stock
Glittered holly berries and
    leaves patterned paper
2 gold brads
Green raffia
Glue stick
Hole punch
Computer font (optional)

A Friend Defined

Design by MARY AYRES

Hemp cord strung through eyelets set on a woodgrain background creates a friendship card with a masculine feel.

MATERIALS

Light brown and dark
   brown card stock
White vellum
Hemp cord
4 black photo corners
2 x 3¼-inch vertical photo
14 (⅛-inch) round antique
   gold eyelets
Brown and black ink pads
Friendship sentiment rub-
   on transfer
Wood grain texture
   embossing plate
Large tip embossing tool
Craft sponge
⅛-inch hole punch
Rotary tool and scoring
   blade
Instant-dry paper adhesive

Cut a 5 x 8½-inch rectangle from light brown card stock; score and fold in half. Tear a 3¾ x 5-inch rectangle from dark brown card stock; apply black ink to edges with craft sponge and adhere to card. Cut a 3½ x 4¾-inch rectangle from light brown card stock; use texture plate to emboss vertical wood grain onto rectangle. Apply brown ink to edges and surface of embossed rectangle; glue rectangle to torn rectangle.

Attach black corners to photo; adhere toward top of embossed rectangle. Punch two ⅛-inch holes ¼ inch apart around each photo corner; attach eyelets.

Transfer friendship sentiment onto vellum; tear a ⅝ x 4-inch rectangle around sentiment and apply brown ink to edges. Place vellum sentiment underneath photo; punch a hole in each corner and punch two holes underneath sentiment. Attach eyelets. Insert hemp cord in and out through eyelets; bring cord ends up through bottom holes and tie a knot at center. Trim ends. ■

SOURCES: Rub-on transfer from Royal & Langnickel; texture embossing plate and embossing tool from Fiskars; Zip Dry paper adhesive from Beacon.

Best Wishes Card

Design by PARIS DUKES, *courtesy of Hot Off The Press*

A simple birthday card gets dressed up for the occasion with ribbon and wire spirals.

Position card with fold at top; use glue stick to adhere olive green patterned paper to front leaving the edges unglued. Cut a 3¼-inch-wide piece of off-white patterned paper and adhere to right side of card; trim edges even.

Mount pre-embossed images onto green vellum; trim leaving small borders. Referring to photo for placement, attach two gold swirl clips to birthday cake image. Use adhesive foam tape to attach cake image to center of card and to help hold swirl clips in place. String fibers through gold clips; wrap ends around to back of paper and tape ends to secure. Adhere paper edges with glue stick.

Add a swirl clip to the bottom left corner of the "Best Wishes" image; attach image with adhesive foam tape to the lower left corner of birthday cake.

For the inside, cut a 2½ x 3¼-inch piece of olive green patterned paper; cut a piece of off-white patterned paper the same size. Line up both pieces inside card and adhere. Cut out birthday sentiment quote and mount onto green vellum; trim leaving a small border and adhere on top of patterned papers. ■

SOURCES: Patterned papers, vellum, fibers, gold clips, pre-embossed birthday images and birthday quote from Hot Off The Press.

MATERIALS

- 5 x 6½-inch blank white card
- Olive green and off-white patterned paper
- Green vellum
- Pre-embossed birthday cake and "Best Wishes" images
- Birthday sentiment quote
- Green fibers
- 3 gold swirl clips
- Tape
- Adhesive foam tape
- Glue stick

Dream Dancer Pendant

Design by SUSAN HUBER

A selection of beads and artful fibers grace the pendant of this elegantly retro necklace!

MATERIALS

- Vintage lady dancer image
- Light brown antique-finish ink pad
- 2 (1 x 3-inch) glass slides
- Copper foil tape
- Soldering flux
- Lead free solder
- Square jump rings: 2 large and 5 small
- Triangle jump rings: 2 small and 1 large
- 3 eye pins
- Assorted beads
- Red fibers
- Small holding clamp
- Soldering iron
- Stipple brush
- Craft knife
- Needle-nose pliers

Use stipple brush to lightly apply light brown ink to lady dancer image; cut image to fit glass slides and insert image between slides. Beginning from the bottom edge, apply the copper foil tape around the glass edges. **Note:** *Do not fold over the foil tape edges until tape has been applied to the entire perimeter.* Beginning on the sides, fold down tape edges; fold the bottom and top edges. Smooth out wrinkles making sure tape is well sealed to glass slides. Cut away excess tape with a craft knife.

Hold glass slide with small holding clamp. Apply a layer of flux onto the top edge of the glass slide. Place hot soldering iron tip onto top edge; place solder against the tip and let the solder melt and run down iron tip onto copper surface. Slowly move iron tip and melting solder along top edge until edge is completely covered; continue applying flux and solder to remaining edges. Smooth any rough areas or bumps with hot iron tip.

To attach a large square jump ring, melt a small amount of solder at top of slide. Apply flux to the jump ring in the area it will be attached; hold jump ring with needle-nose pliers on area and melt solder. Hold still until solder sets which only takes a few seconds. Repeat steps to add one large and two small square jump rings at bottom of slide.

Thread desired beads onto eye pins; create a loop on ends to secure beads. Attach remaining square and triangle jump rings to beaded eye pins. Thread fibers through triangle jump rings; attach eye pins to jump rings on soldered slide. Cut desired length of red fiber and thread through top jump ring; tie a knot at top. ■

SOURCES: Distress ink by Ranger; glass slides, lead free solder, soldering flux, soldering iron and foil tape from Scrap a Latte; jump rings from Making Memories.

Dog Days of Summer

Design by KATHLEEN PANEITZ

Perky polka-dotted ribbon accents the simple backstitched letters on this fun card.

MATERIALS

Pewter soft metal sheet
Red vellum
Yellow and white card
     stock
Square pattern embossing
     tool
Metal dog embellishment
Black fine-tip marker
2 orange buttons
Red embroidery floss
Square metal-edge vellum
     tag
Paw print punch
Black polka-dot ribbon
Sewing needle
Needle tool
Mouse pad
Vellum tape
Tape
Adhesive foam tape
Adhesive dots

Cut yellow card stock 5 x 10⅜ inches; score and fold in half. Cut a 4⅝ x 2⅜-inch piece of pewter metal sheet; run piece through square pattern embossing tool and adhere toward top of card.

Cut white card stock 4⅝ x 2½ inches; lightly pencil "Dog days" onto card stock leaving room for remaining words. Place card stock onto mouse pad and use needle tool to punch holes for sewing in letters. Thread sewing needle with red embroidery floss and stitch letters; secure ends on back with tape. Use black fine-tip marker to write "Bask in the" above letters and "of summer" below letters. Adhere sewn card stock to bottom portion of card.

Cut a 4⅝-inch length of black polka-dot ribbon; adhere to card where metal and card stock meet. Attach buttons to left side of ribbon with adhesive dots.

Cut a 2 x 2¼-inch piece of red vellum; attach metal dog embellishment to vellum with adhesive foam tape. Attach vellum to upper right corner of card. Punch a paw print from yellow card stock and adhere to metal-edge tag. Attach tag in upper left corner. ■

SOURCES: Art Emboss metal sheet from AMACO; Li'l Boss embossing tool from Paper Adventures; metal dog embellishment from Pilgrim Imports; vellum tag from Making Memories; Paw print punch from Plaid/All Night Media.

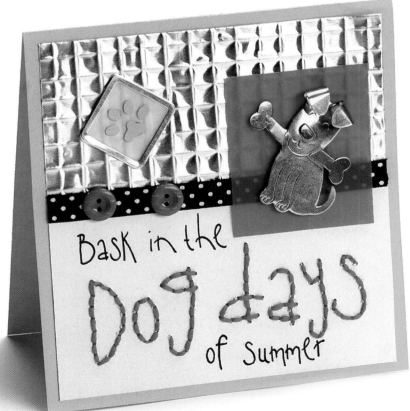

I Love Paris

Design by SUSAN STRINGFELLOW

Show your feelings about this great city with a tag that proclaims your love!

Paint chipboard tag with a coat of black paint, a coat of crackle medium and a coat of white paint, allowing each coat to dry thoroughly before applying another. Dab a sponge lightly onto brown ink pad and rub over surface of tag. Cut and tear strips of patterned papers; adhere strips randomly to tag.

Stamp Eiffel Tower image onto tag using black solvent-based ink; attach French postage stamp. Using black solvent-based ink, stamp "Journey of the Heart" toward top of tag and decorative background image along left side of tag.

Cut a 9-inch piece of striped ribbon; cut a 4-inch piece of sheer black ribbon. Wrap striped ribbon around bottom portion of tag and tie; tie sheer ribbon around striped ribbon and tie. Trim ribbon ends in V-notches.

Lay "Paris" transparency toward top of tag and attach with adhesive metal word embellishment. Use a small piece of adhesive foam tape to attach "I" letter sticker above metal word embellishment. Attach silk 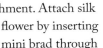 flower by inserting mini brad through center.

Cut ten 6-inch lengths of fibers; insert fiber ends through hole and back through formed loop. Pull taut. ■

SOURCES: Chipboard tag from Paperbilities; patterned papers from Anna Griffin Inc.; decorative background and Eiffel Tower rubber stamps from Stampabilities; PSX "Journey of the Heart" stamp from Duncan; solvent-based ink pad from Tsukineko; metal word embellishment from Marcella by Kay/Target; patterned papers, Paris transparency and French postage stamp from Altered Pages; mini brad from Making Memories; letter sticker from EK Success.

MATERIALS

Chipboard tag
Floral and ivory patterned
    papers
Fibers: black, pink
    and cream
1½-inch-wide black and
    white striped ribbon
⅜-inch-wide sheer
    black ribbon
Rubber stamps: decorative
    background, Eiffel
    tower and "Journey of
    the Heart"
Self-adhesive "love" metal
    word embellishment
"Paris" transparency
"I" letter sticker
French postage stamp
Silk flower
Black mini brad
Black and white acrylic
    paint
Crackle medium
Black solvent-based ink
    pad
Brown ink pad
Paintbrush
Craft sponge
Glue stick
Adhesive foam dots

Star Gift Bags DIAGRAMS ON PAGE 92

Design by HELEN RAFSON

Embroidered motifs dress up gift bags for an all-star occasion.

MATERIALS

4 x 5¼-inch white gift bag
5¼ x 8½-inch light blue
    gift bag
Red corrugated paper
    Variegated blue
    embroidery floss
3 (6mm) gold jump rings
    3 small gold star charms
5 (7mm) clear rhinestones
4 inches ⅝-inch-wide red,
    white and blue striped
    ribbon
23 inches 1-inch-wide red,
    white and blue striped
    ribbon
Black fine-tip permanent
    marker
Sewing needle
Needle-nose pliers
Instant-hold glue
Instant-dry paper adhesive
Gem adhesive

Star Gift Bag

Use pattern provided to trace and cut a small star from red corrugated paper. Mark dots between ridges ⅛ inch from edge around perimeter of star. Make holes at dots with sewing needle. Thread needle with variegated blue floss and stitch straight stitches vertically between ridges. Glue ends of floss to back of star; let dry.

Draw stitch marks around front of bag with fine-tip marker. Use sewing needle to make three holes at top of bag for star charms. Attach jump rings to charms with needle-nose pliers; attach jump rings through holes at top of bag.

Adhere ⅝-inch-wide striped ribbon across top of bag underneath charms with instant-hold glue. Use paper adhesive to glue star onto bag; let dry.

Stars & Rhinestones Gift Bag

Use patterns provided to trace and cut a small and large star from red corrugated paper. Following instructions above, stitch variegated floss onto stars. Glue stars onto light blue gift bag with paper adhesive. Use gem adhesive to glue clear rhinestones randomly around stars. Tie a bow onto bag handle with 1-inch-wide striped ribbon. ∎

SOURCES: Corrugated paper and gift bag from DMD, Inc.; Kid's Choice Glue and Paper-Tac adhesive from Beacon.

Snowflake Tag

Design by DEANNA HUTCHISON

Create dozens of these quick and easy tags to adorn all your holiday packages!

MATERIALS

Light blue and white card stock
Blue patterned paper
White vellum
3 silver brads
White sheer ribbon
Snowflake punch
Hole punch
Glue stick

Cut light blue card stock 2⅝ x 4½ inches; cut top two corners to from a tag shape. Cut blue patterned paper 2½ x 4½ inches; cut top two corners to form a tag and tear bottom edge. Adhere to light blue tag.

Cut three 1-inch squares from blue patterned paper; mount each onto light blue card stock. Trim edges leaving a narrow border. Mount again onto white card stock and trim leaving a narrow border.

Punch three snowflakes from vellum and attach one to each layered square with silver brads. Adhere squares across tag. Punch two holes at top of tag. Beginning from the front, insert ribbon ends through holes. Cross ends over each other and thread back through holes bringing ends to front. ∎

SOURCES: Snowflake punch from Emagination Crafts.

Beaded Tree Tag

Design by DEANNA HUTCHISON

Beads strung on wire wrapped around a simple die-cut tree sparkle in the holiday lights!

Cut a 2½ x 4-inch rectangle from green card stock; tear two small strips of clear vellum and attach to bottom of green rectangle with vellum tape. Trim edges. Adhere green piece to a 2¾ x 4¼-inch piece of red card stock.

Punch a tree shape from dark green card stock; wrap wire around tree and thread on clear seed beads randomly. Secure wire ends in back with adhesive dots. Punch three holes for snowflake eyelets toward top of rectangle; attach eyelets. Use adhesive foam tape to attach tree to rectangle.

Use glue stick to adhere assembled piece onto a 3½ x 5-inch piece of white card stock; tear edges. Punch a hole at top; thread red and white ribbon ends through hole and back through formed loop. ■

SOURCES: Tree punch from Emagination Crafts.

MATERIALS

Card stock: red, dark
   green, green and white
White vellum
Silver craft wire
Clear seed beads
3 snowflake eyelets
Red and white sheer
   ribbon
Tree punch
Hole punch
Vellum tape
Adhesive dots
Adhesive foam tape
Glue stick

Vibrant Reflections

Design by MARY LYNN MALONEY

Shimmering papers and fibers magically create the appearance of reflections in a mountain stream.

Cover work surface with several sheets of scrap paper; lay handmade paper face down onto work surface with 12-inch side positioned toward top. Spray upper half of paper with adhesive. Open envelope flap and lay envelope vertically onto sprayed area of handmade paper with top of envelope approximately 2 inches beneath top of paper. Fold 2-inch extended paper over inside envelope flap clipping curved areas to fit.

Spray bottom half of handmade paper with adhesive; fold paper up and adhere around envelope. Smooth and trim paper making sure entire envelope is covered. Fold excess paper inside envelope. Use craft knife and metal-edge ruler to trim long sides leaving ¼-inch border on both sides; save trimmed paper.

Cut a 2½ x 9-inch rectangle from royal blue textured card stock; using envelope flap as a pattern, cut a flap shape from royal blue rectangle. Use spray adhesive to wrap a piece of remaining handmade paper around curved edge of blue card stock. Adhere blue flap to the underside of envelope flap as an extension. Open envelope flap; machine-sew a straight stitch down both long sides of envelope with dark red thread. Trim threads.

Use spray adhesive to cover buttons with scraps of handmade paper; apply a small amount of fabric adhesive onto each button. Wrap buttons randomly with various fibers; trim fiber ends and let dry. Use adhesive foam dots to attach a button to the center of envelope flap and another button approximately 1 inch below envelope flap.

Cut a 20-inch piece of desired fiber; apply a very small amount of fabric adhesive around the underside of top button. Tie fiber tightly around the underside of button letting remaining fiber dangle.

Punch three holes along the bottom edge of envelope; cut 12 lengths of remaining fibers and loop four through each hole letting fibers dangle. ∎

SOURCES: Spray adhesive from Krylon; Fabri-Tac adhesive from Beacon.

MATERIALS

- 9 x 12-inch envelope
- 12 x 30-inch lightweight multicolor handmade paper
- 8 x 10-inch royal blue textured card stock
- Scrap paper
- 2 (1-inch diameter) flat-backed buttons
- 3 yards metallic fibers
- 3 yards assorted fuzzy and soft fibers
- ⅛-inch hole punch
- Sewing machine with dark red sewing thread
- Craft knife
- Metal-edge ruler
- Toothpick
- 2 (½-inch diameter) adhesive foam dots
- Spray adhesive
- Fabric adhesive

Fairy Dust Pin

Design by TRACEY OLSON

Transform an ordinary piece of cardboard into a stunning fashion accessory with gold embossing enamel and sparkling metallic fibers.

MATERIALS

Metallic fibers

2³/₈-inch square cardboard

Gold fairy charm

Gold ultra thick embossing enamel

Gold micro beads

Watermark ink pad

3–4 various pearlescent pigment powders

Pin back

¹/₈- and ¹/₄-inch hole punches

Heat embossing tool

Sponge-tip applicator

Flat container

Punch one ¼-inch and three ⅛-inch holes in one corner of cardboard square. Coat the entire surface of square with a large amount of watermark ink. Pour gold ultra thick embossing enamel into flat container; set aside. Cover cardboard square with gold embossing enamel and emboss.

Immediately after embossing enamel has melted, place square face down into the embossing enamel in container. Continue to emboss gold enamel until there are four layers of embossing enamel on square. Allow each coat to melt completely.

Use sponge-tip applicator to apply pearlescent pigment powders onto square in desired pattern. Reheat embossed square until enamel and pigment powders melt; immediately sprinkle micro beads onto square in various areas. Reheat center of square until melted and immediately place fairy charm onto square; press down slightly. Loop several metallic fibers through punched holes; attach pin back to back of square. ∎

SOURCES: Fairy charm by Talisman Artifacts; Pearl Ex powders from Jacquard Products; watermark ink pad from Tsukineko.

Amy's Address Book

Design by SUSAN STRINGFELLOW

Transform an ordinary store-bought address book into a something special with fun fibers and papers that reflect your personal style.

MATERIALS

Spiral bound address book
Card stock: blue, orange,
   dark pink and pink
Multicolor striped paper
Pink party glasses
   patterned paper
Pastel and metallic fibers
Friend definition rubber
   stamp
Alphabet rubber stamps
Black and clear embossing
   ink pads
White embossing powder
Flower and leaf buttons
"Giggle" metal circle tag
Small silver brad
Sheer green polka-dot
   ribbon
Sewing machine with
   white sewing thread
Embossing heat tool
Sanding block
Glue stick
Craft glue

Cut a piece of blue card stock to fit front cover of address book; lightly sand edges. Cut a 3 x 7-inch piece of striped paper and adhere to left side of blue card stock piece approximately ¼ inch from edge. Cut a 2½ x 3-inch piece of pink party glasses patterned paper; adhere toward lower right corner of card stock. Use zigzag stitch to machine-sew along left edge of striped paper; straight stitch around pink party glasses patterned paper. Attach sewn card stock to front of address book.

Stamp friend definition image onto pink card stock with clear embossing ink; emboss with white embossing powder. Cut out image; sand edges and mat onto orange card stock. Adhere in upper left corner of book.

Cut a small strip of pink card stock; sand edges and attach horizontally in lower left corner of book. Glue flower and leaf buttons on top of pink strip. Tie a small piece of sheer green ribbon through metal circle tag and adhere toward upper right corner; glue a flower and leaf button overlapping circle tag.

Use alphabet rubber stamps and black ink to stamp "addresses" vertically along right side of book; stamp desired name horizontally onto striped paper. Cut a small piece of sheer green ribbon; fold in half and attach above "addresses" with small silver brad.

Cut several 4-inch lengths of pastel and metallic fibers; wrap fibers around spiral binding and tie knots. ■

SOURCES: Patterned paper from Doodlebug Design Inc.; patterned paper from Treehouse Designs; rubber stamps from Hero Arts; "Giggle" tag from Colorbök; sanding block from PM Designs.

friend (frĕnd) n. 1. A person whom one knows, likes, and trusts. 2. A favored companion. —be friends with. To be a friend of. —make friends with. To befriend. friend·ly (frĕnd'lē) adj. -lier, -liest. 1. Of, pertaining to, or befitting a friend. 2. Favorably disposed. 3. Warm; comforting. 4. On terms of friendship.

Chocolate Tag

DIAGRAMS ON PAGE 93

Design by SUSAN BASCOM

Soft, white fibers are ideal for embellishing this cup of steamy hot chocolate. Attach the tag to packets of flavored cocoa for a quick gift!

MATERIALS

Ivory tag

White card stock

White vellum

White and metallic fibers

Brown chalk

Craft sponge

Multicolor embossing
   powder

Computer font or
   embossing ink pen

Embossing heat tool

Industrial-strength double-
   sided tape

Glue pen

Use craft sponge to apply brown chalk to the edges of the ivory tag. Draw swirls toward top portion of tag with glue pen; adhere white fibers onto swirls to represent steam. Use a computer or hand-print with embossing ink pen "Hot Chocolate" onto vellum; emboss with multicolor embossing powder. Trim a rectangle around embossed words and adhere over white fibers.

Cut and attach pieces of industrial-strength double-sided tape to form a 1½-inch square toward bottom of tag. Cover tape with strands of metallic fibers until no tape or paper can be seen through fibers.

Use patterns provided to cut out teacup, handle and saucer from white card stock. Draw glue lines around teacup rim and saucer; adhere metallic fibers to glue. Assemble teacup and saucer; adhere on top of metallic fibers. ∎

SOURCES: Embossing powder from Uptown Design Co.; double-sided tape from Magic Scraps.

Blooming Tissue Topper

Design by SUSAN STRINGFELLOW

Decoupage, rubber stamping and a hint of sparkling fibers come together on this tissue topper to create sophisticated home decor.

Adhere patterned paper to tissue box cover using decoupage medium; trim excess paper. Attach one tall flower image to each side of box; apply a coat of decoupage medium to entire surface and let dry. Rub box with brown ink pad to give an antique appearance.

Use sponge brush to apply gold paint to decorative foam stamp; stamp image along some of the side and top edges. Let dry. Attach desired floral stickers; attach letter stickers to spell "Bloom" vertically along one side of box. Adhere metallic gold fibers around opening and base. ∎

SOURCES: Papier-mâché tissue box cover from Walnut Hollow; patterned paper and flower images from K&Company; decorative foam stamp from Making Memories; Matte Decoupage Medium from Golden Artist Colors.

MATERIALS

- Papier-mâché tissue box cover
- Metallic gold fibers
- Tan swirl patterned paper
- Tall flower images
- Coordinating floral stickers
- Letter stickers
- Brown ink pad
- Decorative swirl foam stamp
- Gold acrylic paint
- Decoupage medium
- Sponge brush

Cheetah CD

Design by SUSAN STRINGFELLOW

Take a walk on the wild side when you display this CD embellished with rubberstamped images of African animals and tribal motifs.

MATERIALS

Blank compact disc
Brown patterned paper
Metallic gold and green
    patterned paper
Light green textured paper
Brown mesh
Scrap piece of card stock
Brown polymer clay
Cheetah rubber stamp
African background
    rubber stamp
Black solvent-based
ink pad
Copper metallic rub-on
    cream
Fibers: brown, green and
    metallic copper
Brown and amber beaded
    fringe trim
Gold sewing thread
Sewing needle
Sandpaper
Craft knife
Rolling pin
Wooden dowel
Magnets
Clear dimensional
    adhesive

Lightly sand the front and back of CD. Lay CD onto brown patterned paper and cut around it with craft knife. Stamp the African background image along the right edge of paper with black solvent-based ink; adhere to CD.

Cut a 1-inch-wide strip of metallic gold and green patterned paper; apply black ink to edges and adhere down left side of CD. Trim excess paper. Cut a 3 x 2½-inch piece of light green textured paper; tear one short edge. Cut a 3-inch piece of beaded trim and attach to the lower backside of the textured paper; adhere to left side of CD.

Roll out polymer clay to ⅛-inch thickness. Use black solvent-based ink to stamp cheetah and three separate images from African background stamp into clay. Cut images out and gently shape as desired. Bake according to package directions and allow to cool completely. ***Note:*** *Make two holes on left side of cheetah image with wooden dowel before baking.* Rub clay surfaces lightly with black solvent-based ink and copper metallic cream.

Cut a 1½ x 2-inch piece of mesh; lay it on top of green textured paper where cheetah image will be attached. Cut four 5-inch pieces of green and copper metallic fibers; thread fibers through cheetah image and attach to CD with clear dimensional adhesive. Adhere brown fibers around perimeter of CD.

Cut a small piece of mesh and lay it in lower right corner where two small clay images will be attached. Use clear dimensional adhesive to attach one clay image in upper left corner and two clay images in lower right corner on top of mesh.

For tassel, wrap several lengths of green and copper metallic fibers around a 2-inch-wide piece of card stock; thread a 2-inch-long piece of copper fiber through one side of wrapped fibers and tie a knot. Trim fiber ends. Cut other side of fibers; trim tassel to desired length. Thread sewing needle with gold thread and wrap thread several times around tassel ¼ inch from top; tie a knot and run needle through the center of wrapped tassel. Trim thread. Tie tassel to fibers at bottom of CD. Glue two magnets to back. ∎

SOURCES: Textured paper from ProvoCraft; rubber stamps from Stampin' Up! and Addicted to Rubber Stamps; solvent-based ink pad from Tsukineko; brown mesh from Magenta; Diamond Glaze dimensional adhesive from JudiKins.

Silver Sparkle Bookmark

Design by LAURIE D'AMBROSIO

Weave metallic fibers through paper punched holes for a stylish edging that will add a classy touch to an ordinary bookmark.

MATERIALS

Metallic silver and navy blue card stock
⅛-inch-wide silver ribbon
Silver medium braid
Diamond border punch
Square punch
Adhesive dots
Mini adhesive dots

Cut two pieces of metallic silver card stock, one measuring 2⅛ x 5⅛ inches and the other 1⅛ x 4¾ inches. Cut a 2⅛ x 4¾-inch piece of navy blue card stock; punch long sides of navy blue piece with diamond border.

Cut four 7-inch pieces of ⅛-inch-wide silver ribbon; weave ribbon in and out through the punched diamonds. Secure ends on back with mini adhesive dots; trim excess.

Adhere the small piece of silver card stock on top of navy blue piece; mount piece onto large silver piece and punch a hole at top. Cut two 10-inch pieces of medium braid and three 10-inch pieces of silver ribbon; loop braid and ribbons through hole. If needed, secure loop with a mini adhesive dot. ■

SOURCES: Ribbon and medium braid from Kreinik; border and square punches from Fiskars.

Rising Sun Keychain

Design by LISA ROJAS

Paper glaze turns a simple rubberstamped image into a keychain tag. Assorted fibers and beads add the finishing touch for this project!

Trace tag onto mat board and white card stock; cut out tags. Stamp sun and clouds image onto white card-stock tag; add color with pastel chalks and apply preservative spray. After tag has dried, glue tag to mat board tag with clear gel tacky glue.

Spread a layer of paper glaze over top of tag; let dry. Wrap double-sided tape around edges and dip edges into silver embossing powder; emboss with heat tool. Paint back of tag metallic silver; let dry. Loop several fibers through hole and tie on key ring; thread sun charm and beads onto fibers. ∎

SOURCES: Aleene's Paper Glaze and Aleene's Clear Gel Tacky Glue from Duncan; Super Tape from Therm O Web; preservative spray from Krylon; pastel chalks from Loew-Cornell; rubber stamp from Plaid/All Night Media.

MATERIALS

2 x 3¾-inch tag
Mat board
White card stock
Sun and clouds rubber
    stamp
Black ink pad
Silver embossing powder
Pastel chalks
Silver key ring
Assorted blue beads
Blue fibers
Sun charm
Metallic silver acrylic paint
Preservative spray
Dimensional glaze
Clear gel tacky glue
Heat embossing tool
Craft knife
Paintbrush
Double-stick embossable
    tape

Dance Like No One's Watching CD

Design by TRACEY OLSON

Create this stunning CD to remind yourself or someone special to enjoy every moment of life to the fullest.

Use makeup wedge to spread an even layer of pink pearlescent paint on top of CD; let dry. Ink one of the sentiment stamps with black solvent-based ink and stamp on top half of CD making sure to press down evenly and hard. Repeat clockwise around CD with remaining sentiment stamps.

Starting from the back of the CD, adhere fibers with double-sided tape; run fibers through center hole. Twist and adhere fibers down the bottom of the CD. Cut desired length of fiber for hanger and thread through attached fibers on reverse side of CD; secure fibers with double-sided tape and knot at top.

Tear out dancer image and apply pink chalk to edges with sponge-tip applicator; adhere image over center hole with double-sided tape.

Rub pink metallic cream onto fairy charm; attach charm to fibers with pink jump ring. Close jump ring securely with needle-nose pliers. Use battery etcher engraver or an ice pick to etch "LOVE" onto clear stone; adhere a small scrap of metallic red paper to back of stone and glue to CD. Apply glitter glue along left edge of CD; use blue metallic rub-on cream along right edge. ∎

SOURCES: Dancer image from Altered Pages; solvent-based ink pad from Tsukineko; Lumiere pearlescent paint from Jacquard Products; fairy charm from Talisman Artifacts.

MATERIALS

Blank compact disc
Pink and red metallic
 fibers
Rubber stamps: love,
 sing, live and dance
 sentiments
Dancer image
Scrap piece of metallic red
 paper
Black solvent-based ink
 pad
Clear stone
Pink jump ring
Small fairy charm
Pearlescent pink paint
Pink chalk
Blue and pink metallic
 rub-on cream
Glitter glue
Double-sided tape
Gem adhesive
Sponge-tip applicator
Makeup wedge
Battery etcher engraver or
 ice pick
Needle-nose pliers

Crazy Quilt Journal

Design by LAURIE D'AMBROSIO

Iron-on fibers adorn the cover of this journal to create a charming patchwork look.

MATERIALS

6 x 8-inch scrapbook

Assorted textured and patterned papers

Ivory card stock

Computer printer paper

1/8-inch-wide iron-on ribbon: gold, green and copper

Medium and fine braid fibers in desired colors

Black twisted silk fiber

Assorted tags and art images

Pearl covered buttons

White button

Mini iron

Heat-resistant cloth

Button shank remover

Sewing needle

Small tip scissors

1/8-inch hole punch

Mini adhesive dots

Adhesive dots

Cut two 7 x 5¾-inch pieces of computer printer paper; cut a piece of ivory card stock the same size. Cut pieces of computer paper into various size shapes; arrange shapes onto ivory card stock piece until a pleasing arrangement has been created. Use pieces as templates to cut out textured and patterned papers. Adhere papers to ivory card stock with adhesive dots to form the "quilt."

Punch 1/8-inch holes in desired areas on quilt where stitching will be. Use sewing needle and choice of fibers to sew zigzag, straight or cross-stitches in chosen areas. Secure ends in back with mini adhesive dots.

Following manufacturer's instructions, iron-on gold, green and copper ribbons in desired areas. Add gold iron-on ribbon as a border around entire piece. ***Note:*** *Wrap heat-resistant cloth around mini iron when ironing so adhesive does not stick to iron.* Use mini adhesive dots to add fibers that are not iron-on.

Punch two holes and stitch on white button where desired; remove shanks from pearl-covered buttons and attach with adhesive dots. Cut out selected art images and adhere to quilt. Punch holes in tags; loop fibers through holes and attach to quilt. Attach assembled quilt to front of book with adhesive dots. Tie a bow with several fibers; attach to quilt with mini adhesive dot.

Cut several 10½-inch pieces of fibers; hold fibers together and tie a knot in one end. Wrap remaining end around book spiral and tie a knot to create a connected bookmark. ■

SOURCES: Textured and patterned papers and scrapbook from DMD, Inc.; fibers and iron-on ribbons from Kreinik; Buttons and button shanker remover from Blumenthal Lansing.

ALWAYS MAINTAIN A KIND OF SUMMER

EVEN IN THE MIDDLE OF WINTER.
-HENRY DAVID THOREAU.

Maintain a Kind of Summer CD

Design by TRACEY OLSON

Gold leaf and sparkling embossing powder will give you summer's warmth all year round.

Paint CD metallic green; let dry. Spread an even layer of pearlescent turquoise paint over metallic paint with makeup wedge; let dry completely. Ink word background image with watermark ink pad and stamp onto right half of CD; emboss area with gold embossing powder. ***Note:*** *Slowly move embossing heat tool when embossing CD so as not to warp the CD. If CD begins to warp, place a heavy object such as a book on top of it until it has cooled.*

Hold fibers together and tape ends in back on the bottom of the CD; thread fibers through the center hole and wind them up over the top. Bring them back through the hole and wind them back around to back; thread them through the hole again and let fibers dangle.

Apply foil glue to top side of the slide mount; let dry until glue is tacky. Use a stiff paintbrush to apply the gold leaf to slide mount until surface is completely covered. Use soft paintbrush to lightly brush away excess gold leaf flakes.

Stamp summer quote onto white and gold patterned papers with black ink pad; cut quote into two strips. Use double-sided tape to attach first half of quote angled in top left portion of CD; fold paper edges around to back. Attach second strip in same manner toward bottom of CD.

Lay desired photo on the backside of slide mount so it shows through opening. Place two layers of mounting tape on the top and bottom of the backside of slide mount; attach over center hole on CD. Cut off metal stem on brads with wire cutters; cut an adhesive dot into four pieces and use them to attach the brads to left side of CD. Adhere dragonfly button to right side of CD with double-sided tape. Attach magnet to back of CD. ■

SOURCES: Rubber stamps from PSX and Uptown Design Co.; patterned papers from NRN Designs; slide mount and double-sided tape from Altered Pages; watermark ink pad from Tsukineko; Lumiere pearlescent turquoise paint from Jacquard Products; Amy's Magic Gold Leaf and foil glue from Scrapgoods; acrylic paint from Plaid.

MATERIALS

- Blank compact disc
- Assorted metallic and nonmetallic fibers
- Gold and white patterned papers
- Word background rubber stamp
- Summer quote rubber stamp
- Slide mount
- Small square brads: 2 white and 2 mint green
- Black ink pad
- Watermark ink pad
- Gold embossing powder
- Gold leaf
- Dragonfly button
- Metallic green acrylic paint
- Pearlescent turquoise paint
- Small photo
- Large magnet
- Makeup wedge
- Embossing heat tool
- Sponge brush
- Stiff and soft paintbrushes
- Wire cutters
- Foil glue
- Tape
- Mounting tape

Gone Fishing Frame

Design by SUSAN STRINGFELLOW

Assorted metallic fibers replicate lures used on a memorable fishing trip. Cork letters make it easy to personalize this frame!

Use decoupage medium to adhere green patterned paper to frame; sponge edges of frame with brown ink. Cut three 2-inch squares from light brown card stock; tear one edge on each. Dampen the squares lightly and crumple up. Microwave crumpled squares on high for approximately thirty seconds or let air-dry. Uncrumple squares and sponge with brown ink; attach along right side of frame.

Cut a 1 x 6-inch piece of natural mesh; attach along bottom of frame overlapping brown square. Cut two 1½-inch squares from natural mesh; attach to top two squares.

Stamp fish image onto off-white card stock with brown ink; paint fish with walnut ink. Once image is dry, punch fish into three 1¼-inch squares; sponge edges with brown ink and attach one square to each of the three brown card stock squares.

Stamp "Gone Fishing" onto medium cork rectangle with black solvent-based ink; sponge brown ink on edges. Cut several 7-inch lengths of metallic fibers; attach to left side of cork rectangle with bronze brad. Adhere tag in upper left corner of frame.

Stamp "AND" onto small cork rectangle with black solvent-based ink; sponge edges with brown ink. Attach cork letters and small rectangle to bottom of frame to spell desired names.

Create a small fish hook from bronze wire; wrap top of hook with metallic fibers and tie into a knot to create the look of a fishing fly. Glue fish hook and mini fishing-themed ornaments to top and middle brown squares. ■

SOURCES: Patterned paper from EK Success; cork embellishments from LazerLetterz; rubber stamps from PSX and Rubber Stamp Ave.; solvent-based ink pad from Tsukineko; mesh from Magic Mesh; square punch from Creative Memories; Matte Decoupage Medium from Golden Artist Colors.

MATERIALS

Papier-mâché frame
Off-white and light brown
    card stock
Green patterned paper
Cork embellishments:
    letters, small rectangle
    and medium rectangle
Fish rubber stamp
Alphabet rubber stamps
Black solvent-based ink
    pad
Brown ink pad
Assorted metallic fibers
Small fishing-themed
    ornaments
Thin bronze wire
Mini bronze brad
Natural mesh
Walnut ink
Decoupage medium
1¼-inch square punch
Paintbrush
Craft sponge
Microwave (optional)

Someday Sailing Keepsake Box

Design by SUSAN STRINGFELLOW

Treasures from a day on the water will be kept safe inside this charming papier-mâché box decorated with fibers and seaside embellishments.

Use screwdriver to take hinged hardware off box; set aside. Paint box with two coats of sand textured paint; allow to dry. Attach hinged hardware.

Sand edges of lighthouse image and adhere in top left corner of box lid with decoupage medium; apply two coats of decoupage medium to top of box. Mat sailing photo onto white and black card stock; attach eyelets in corners. Use alphabet rubber stamps and black solvent-based ink to stamp desired word onto side of photo. Thread gold fiber through eyelets; attach to box lid securing fiber ends in back with adhesive foam tape.

Fill glass bottle with sand and close with cork stopper; tie to left side of photo with gold fiber. Add a small amount of clear dimensional adhesive to bottle to secure. Adhere several shell beads in lower left corner of lid.

Cut six pieces of fibers 2 inches longer than perimeter of box; braid fibers together and clamp ends with clamshell clips. Wrap around edge of lid and secure with clear dimensional adhesive. ■

SOURCES: Solvent-based ink pad from Tsukineko; lighthouse image and fiber tassie clips from Altered Pages; eyelets from Scraplovers; shell beads from Magic Scraps; Matte decoupage Medium from Golden Artist Colors; Diamond Glaze adhesive from JudiKins; sanding block from PM Designs; alphabet rubber stamps from Hero Arts.

MATERIALS

Papier-mâché hinged box
White and black card stock
Lighthouse image
Small sailing photo
Sand textured paint
Fibers: blue, light blue and metallic gold
Small alphabet rubber stamps
Black solvent-based ink pad
4 small black eyelets
Small shell beads
Small glass bottle with cork stopper
Sand
2 gold clamshell clips
Sanding block
Small screwdriver
Paintbrush
Adhesive foam tape
Decoupage medium
Clear dimensional adhesive

Altered Travel Notes Tin

Design by SAHILY GONZALEZ

Whether the trip takes you around the world or just down the road, create a custom-made tin to hold the photo CDs for each adventure.

MATERIALS

Metal tin

World patterned paper

Stickers: travel-themed, various words, postage stamp and alphabet

Silk flower

Gold brad

Metallic fibers

Small cork rectangles

Alphabet rubber stamps

Black solvent-based ink pad

Blue acrylic paint

Craft sponge

Label maker with label tape

Glue pen

Adhesive dots

Cover front and back of tin with patterned paper using glue pen. Adhere various stickers to front of tin; use glue pen to adhere metallic fibers. Place a brad in the center of silk flower; attach on top of fibers with an adhesive dot.

Sponge the edges of cork rectangles with blue acrylic paint; let dry and glue to top right corner on back of tin. Stamp "my little travel book" onto rectangles with alphabet rubber stamps and black solvent-based ink pad. Attach desired stickers to back of tin. Decorate inside tin as desired with patterned paper, stickers, label maker embellishments, etc. ∎

SOURCES: Patterned paper from Creative Imaginations; stickers from EK Success, Making Memories, NRN Designs, Me & My Big Ideas, Creative Imaginations and Doodlebug Design; cork rectangles from LazerLetterz; PSX rubber stamps from Duncan.

Fun Flip Flop Gift Box

Design by SUSAN STRINGFELLOW

This bright and sunny gift box is the perfect wrap for fun summer accessories.

Trace box lid onto the backside of striped paper; cut out and adhere face up on lid. Cut a 1-inch-wide strip of pink polka-dot paper; adhere to edge of lid and fold edge of strip inside lid. Cut a small piece of pink polka-dot paper and adhere to flip flop strap; fold paper edges underneath strap.

Paint box and inside lid blue; paint underneath flip flop strap pink. Let paint dry and apply two coats of varnish to entire box. Allow each coat to dry thoroughly.

Use mini lime green brad to attach silk flower to flip flop strap. Adhere yellow fibers along top edge of lid and along bottom of box using clear dimensional adhesive. Wrap and adhere several rows of metallic fibers around bottom of box up to the point where box lid will overlap. ∎

SOURCES: Patterned paper from Doodlebug Design Inc.; patterned paper, mini brad and acrylic paint from Making Memories; Diamond Glaze adhesive from JudiKins.

MATERIALS

Papier-mâché flip flop box
Yellow striped paper
Pink polka-dot paper
Blue and pink acrylic paint
Yellow and pastel metallic
    fibers
Silk flower
Mini lime green brad
Varnish
Clear dimensional
    adhesive
Paintbrush

Silver Baubles Christmas Tree

DIAGRAMS ON PAGE 93

Design by KATHLEEN PANEITZ

Stitch the outline of a Christmas tree and decorate with rhinestones for a quick, simple holiday greeting card.

MATERIALS

- White and navy blue card stock
- Silver metallic paper
- Blue mulberry paper
- Silver thread
- Silver star eyelet
- 6 clear rhinestones
- Sewing needle
- Needle tool
- Mouse pad
- Gem adhesive
- Glue stick

Cut silver metallic paper 4⅛ x 8¼ inches; score and fold in half. Cut a 3¾ x 3⅝-inch piece of blue mulberry paper; adhere to card. Wrap silver thread through card and tie into a bow along seam; trim ends.

Use pattern provided to trace a tree onto a 2⅜ x 2⅝-inch piece of navy blue card stock. Lay piece onto mouse pad and use needle tool to pierce holes along tree shape; use sewing needle and double strand of silver thread to stitch tree outline.

Attach star eyelet to top of tree; mat piece onto white card stock trimming edges leaving a small border. Use gem adhesive to adhere clear rhinestones to tree. ■

SOURCES: Silver metallic paper from Daler-Rowney; star eyelet from The Stamp Doctor.

Initial Ornament

Design by SUSAN STRINGFELLOW

Personalize this tag ornament with an initial and the date— they're so easy you'll want to give one to all your family members and friends!

MATERIALS

Chipboard tag
Green and red striped
 paper
Burgundy card stock
Burgundy and beige
 acrylic paint
Crackle medium
Gold cord
Fibers: red, gold
 and green
Gold embroidery thread
3 small gold bells
Initial rubber stamp
Small alphabet rubber
 stamps
Gold embossing powder
Brown solvent-based ink
 pad
Heat embossing tool
Sewing needle
1⁄16-inch hole punch
Paintbrush
Craft sponge
Glue stick
Tape

Apply a coat of burgundy acrylic paint to tag, followed by a coat of crackle medium and a coat of beige acrylic paint; let each coat dry before moving on to the next. Cut a 1 x 2-inch strip of striped paper; adhere horizontally toward bottom of tag. Use craft sponge to apply brown solvent-based ink along tag edges. Punch three 1⁄16-inch holes across bottom of tag.

Stamp initial image onto a piece of burgundy card stock; emboss with gold embossing powder and cut out. Glue to upper portion of tag.

Cut two 6-inch lengths of gold cord; thread gold bells onto one piece and wrap it around middle of tag. Secure cord ends in back with tape. Fold remaining gold cord piece in half and loop through hole at top of tag; tie a knot at ends for hanger.

For tassels, wrap four fibers around a 2-inch strip of card stock until desired thickness is reached. Cut a 4-inch piece of gold cord; slip gold cord under one side of fibers and tie a knot. Trim cord ends. Cut opposite side of fibers and trim tassel to desired length. Repeat for two additional tassels.

Thread sewing needle with gold thread and wrap thread around tassel several times 1⁄4 inch from top. Tie a knot and pull the cord through the middle of the tassel; trim excess thread. Repeat for remaining tassels. Tie each tassel onto bottom holes on tag with gold cord.

Stamp desired last name, "Christmas" and desired year on tag using small alphabet rubber stamps and brown solvent-based ink. ∎

SOURCES: Chipboard tag from MPR Associates Inc.; striped paper from K&Company; rubber stamps from Addicted to Rubber Stamps and Making Memories; solvent-based ink pad from Tsukineko.

Star Gift Bags

CONTINUED FROM PAGE 62

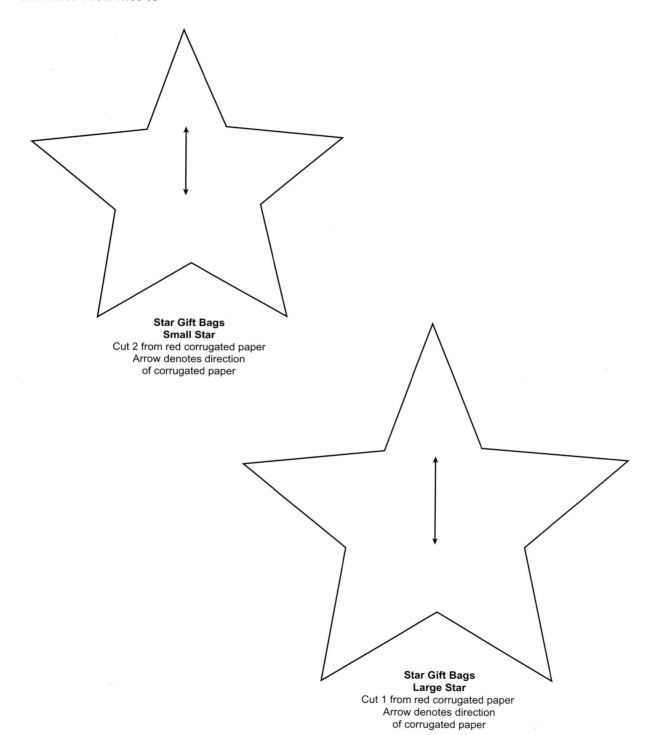

**Star Gift Bags
Small Star**
Cut 2 from red corrugated paper
Arrow denotes direction
of corrugated paper

**Star Gift Bags
Large Star**
Cut 1 from red corrugated paper
Arrow denotes direction
of corrugated paper

Chocolate Tag

CONTINUED FROM PAGE 72

Chocolate Tag
Teacup Handle

Chocolate Tag
Saucer

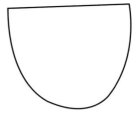

Chocolate Tag
Teacup

Silver Baubles Christmas Tree

CONTINUED FROM PAGE 90

**Silver Baubles Christmas
Tree Pattern**

Butterfly Card and Gift Bag Set

CONTINUED FROM PAGE 17

Butterfly Card & Gift Bag Set
Butterfly
Arrow shows direction
of corrugated paper

Paper Crafting Basics

Paper crafting is easy, creative and fun. Collect basic tools and supplies, learn a few simple terms and techniques, and you're ready to start. The possibilities abound!

Cutting and Tearing

Craft knife, cutting mat Must-have tools. Mat protects work surface, keeps blades from getting dull.

Measure and mark Diagrams show solid lines for cutting, dotted lines for folding.

Other cutters Guillotine and rotary-blade paper cutters, oval and circle cutters, cutters that cut unusual shapes via a gear or cam system, swivel-blade knives that cut along the channels of plastic templates, and die cutting machines (large or small in size and price). Markers that draw as they cut.

Punches Available in hundreds of shapes and sizes ranging from $1/16$ inch to over 3 inches (use for eyelets, lettering, dimensional punch art, and embellishments). Also punches for two-ring, three-ring, coil, comb and disk binding.

Scissors Long and short blades that cut straight or a pattern. Scissors with nonstick coating are ideal for cutting adhesive sheets and tape, bonsai scissors best for cutting rubber or heavy board. Consider comfort—large holes for fingers, soft grips.

Tearing Tear paper for collage, special effects, layering on cards, scrapbook pages and more. Wet a small paintbrush; tear along the wet line for a deckle edge.

Embellishments

If you are not already a pack rat, it is time to start! Embellish projects with stickers, eyelets, brads, nail heads, wire, beads, iron-on ribbon and braid, memorabilia and printed ephemera.

Embossing

Dry embossing Use a light source, stencil, card stock and stylus tool. Add color, or leave raised areas plain.

Heat embossing Use embossing powder, ink, card stock and a heat tool to create raised designs and textures. Powders come in a wide range of colors. Fine grain is called "detail" and heavier called "ultrathick." Embossing powders will not stick to most dye inks—use pigment inks or special clear embossing inks for best results.

Glues and Adhesives

Basics Each glue or adhesive is formulated for a particular use and specified surfaces. Read the label and carefully follow directions, especially those that involve personal safety and health.

Foam tape adds dimension.

Glue dots, adhesive sheets and cartridge type machines quick grab, no drying time needed.

Glue pens Fine line control.

Glue sticks Wide coverage.

Repositionable products Useful for stencils and temporary holding.

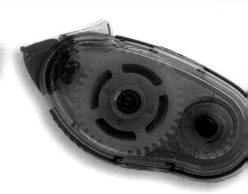

Measuring

Rulers A metal straightedge for cutting with a craft knife (a must-have tool). Match the length of the ruler to the project (shorter rulers are easier to use when working on smaller projects).

Quilter's grid ruler Use to measure squares and rectangles.

Pens and Markers

Choose inks (permanent, watercolor, metallic, etc.), **colors** (sold by sets or individually), **and nibs** (fine point, calligraphy, etc.) **to suit the project.** For journals and scrapbooks, make sure inks are permanent and fade-resistant.

Store pens and markers flat unless the manufacturer says otherwise.

Scoring and Folding

Folding Mountain folds—up, valley folds—down. Most patterns will have different types of dotted lines to denote mountain or valley folds.

Tools Scoring tool and bone folder. Fingernails will scar the surface of the paper.

Paper and Card Stock

Card stock Heavier and stiffer than paper. A sturdy surface for cards, boxes, ornaments.

Paper Lighter weight surfaces used for drawing, stamping, collage.

Storage and organization Store paper flat and away from moisture.

Arrange by color, size or type. Keep your scraps for collage projects.

Types Handmade, milled, marbled, mulberry, origami, embossed, glossy, matte, botanical inclusions, vellum, parchment, preprinted, tissue and more.

Stamping

Direct-to-paper (DTP) Use ink pad, sponge or stylus tool to apply ink instead of a rubber stamp.

Inks Available in pads and re-inker bottles. Types include dye and pigment, permanent, waterproof and fade resistant or archival, chalk finish, fast drying, slow drying, rainbow and more. Read the labels to determine what is best for a project or surface.

Make stamps Carve rubber, erasers, carving blocks, vegetables. Heat Magic Stamp foam blocks to press against textures. Stamp found objects such as leaves and flowers, keys and coins, etc.

Stamps Sold mounted on wood, acrylic or foam, or unmounted (rubber part only), made from vulcanized rubber, acrylic or foam.

Store Flat and away from light and heat.

Techniques Tap the ink onto the stamp (using the pad as the applicator) or tap the stamp onto the ink pad. Stamp with even hand pressure (no rocking) for best results. For very large stamps, apply ink with a brayer. Color the surface of a stamp with watercolor markers (several colors), huff with breath to keep the colors moist, then stamp; or lightly spray with water mist before stamping for a very different effect.

Unmounted stamps Mount temporarily on acrylic blocks with Scotch Poster Tape on one surface (nothing on the rubber stamp) or one of the other methods (hook and loop, paint on adhesives, cling plastic).

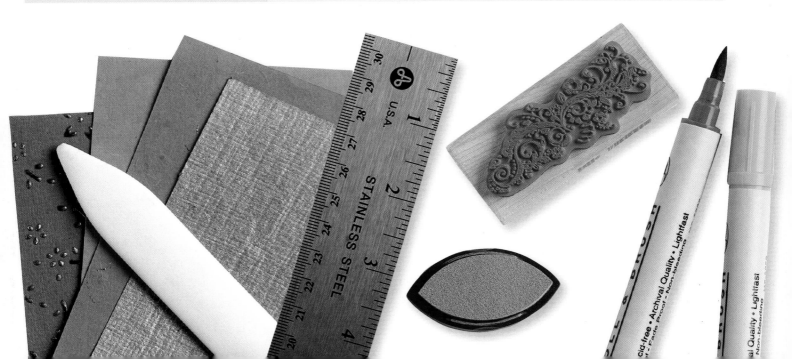

Buyer's Guide

7 Gypsies, (800) 588-6707, www.7gypsies.com

Accent Depot, 1939 Phaeton Ct., Naperville, IL 60565, (630) 548-2133

Addicted to Rubber Stamps, www.addictedtorubberstamps.com

Altered Pages, www.alteredpages.com

American Art Clay Co., 6060 Guion Rd., Indianapolis, IN 46254-1222

Anna Griffin Inc., 733 Lambert Dr., Atlanta, GA 30324, www.annagriffin.com

(The) Artful Lexicon, www.the-artful-lexicon.com

BagWorks Inc., 3301-C S Cravens Rd., Fort Worth, TX 76119

Beacon Adhesives Inc., 125 MacQuestan Pkwy. S., Mount Vernon, NY 10550, (914) 699-3400

The Beadery, P.O. Box 178, Hope Valley, RI 02832, (401) 539-2432

Blumenthal Lansing Co., 1929 Main St., Lansing, IA 52151

Chatterbox, 2141 Beacon Light Rd., Eagle, ID 83616

Clearsnap Inc., P.O. Box 98, Anacortes, WA 98221-0098, (360) 293-6634, www.clearsnap.com

Close To My Heart, 1199 W. 700 S., Pleasant Grove, UT 84062, www.closetomyheart.com

Cloud 9 Design, www.cloud9design.biz

Club Scrap Inc., W6484 Design Drive, Greenville, WI 54942, (888) 634-9100

Craf-T Products, www.craf-tproducts.com

Crafts Etc.!, (800) 888-0321, www.craftsetc.com

Creative Beginnings, www.creativebeginnings.com

Creative Imaginations, 17832 Gothard Street, Hunington Beach, CA 92647, (800) 942-6487

Creative Impressions, 2520 W. Colorado Ave., Colorado Springs, CO 80904, (719) 596-4860

Creative Memories, P.O. Box 1839, 3001 Clearwater Road, St. Cloud, MN 56302-1839, (800) 468-9335

The C-Thru Ruler Co./Deja Views, 6 Britton Dr., Box 356, Bloomfield, CT 06002

Colorbök, www.colorbok.com

Daler-Rowney, www.daler-rowney.com

DecoArt, P.O. Box 386, Stanford, KY 40484, (800) 367-3047

Delta Technical Coatings/Rubber Stampede, 2550 Pellissier Pl., Whittier, CA 90601-1505

Die Cuts with a View, 2250 North University Pkwy., Provo, UT 84604, (801) 224-6766

DMD, Inc., 2300 S. Old Missouri Road, Springdale, AZ 72764, (800) 805-9890

Doodlebug Design Inc., (801) 966-9952, www.doodlebugdesigninc.com

Dow Chemical Co., Customer Information Center, (989) 832-1560

Duncan Enterprises, 5673 E. Shields Ave., Fresno, CA 93727, (800) 438-6226

Dupont, www.dupont.com

Dymo, www.dymo.com

EK Success Ltd., 125 Entin Rd., Clifton, NJ 07014

Emagination Crafts, 463 W. Wrightwood Ave., Elmhurst, IL 60126

Fiskars, 7811 W. Stewart Ave., Wausau, WI 54401-8027

Frances Meyer Inc., P.O. Box 3088, Savannah, GA 31402, (800) 372-6237

Glue Dots International, www.gluedots.com

Golden Artist Colors Inc., 188 Bell Rd., New Berlin, NY 13411-9527, (800) 959-6543

Hero Arts Rubber Stamps, 1343 Powell St., Emeryville, CA 94608

Hirschberg Schutz & Co. Inc., (908) 810-1111

Hot Off The Press Inc., 1250 N.W. Third, Canby, OR 97013

Impress Rubber Stamps, www.impressrubberstamps.com

Jacquard Products: Rupert, Gibbon & Spider, Inc., P.O. Box 425, Healdsburg, CA 95448, (800) 442-0455

Jesse James & Co., 615 N. New St., Allentown, PA 18102

JudiKins, 17803 S. Harvard Blvd., Gardena, CA 90248, (310) 515-1115, www.judikins.com

K&Company, 8500 N.W. River Park Dr., Pillar #136, Parkville, MO 64152

Karen Foster Design, www.scrapbookpaper.com

Keeping Memories Alive, 260 N. Main, Spanish Fork, UT 84660, (800) 419-4949

KI Memories, www.kimemories.com

Kreinik Mfg. Co. Inc., 3106 Lord Baltimore Dr., Suite 101, Baltimore, MD 21244, www.kreinik.com

Krylon/Sherwin-Williams Co., Craft Customer Service, W. 101 Proscpect Ave., Cleveland, OH 44115

LazerLetterz, www.lazerletterz.com

Li'l Davis Designs, 17835 Sky Park Circle, Ste C, Irvine, CA 92614, www.lildavisdesigns.com

Loew-Cornell, 563 Chestnut Ave., Teaneck, NJ 07666-2490

Magenta Rubber Stamps, www.magentarubberstamps.com

Magic Mesh, P.O. Box 8, Lake City, MN 55041, (651) 345-6374

Magic Mounts, P.O. Box 997, 734 Fair Ave. NW, New Philadelphia, OH 44663, (800) 332-0050

Magic Scraps, 1232 Exchange Dr., Richardson, TX 75081

Making Memories, 1168 W. 500 N., Centerville, UT 84014, (801) 294-0430

Me & My Big Ideas, 20321 Valencia Circle, Lake Forest, CA 92630

Michael's, www.michaels.com

MPR Associates Inc., P.O. Box 7343, 529 Townsend Ave., High Point, NC 27264, (800) 334-1047

NRN Designs, www.nrndesigns.com

Offray, R.R. 24, Box 601, Chester, NJ 07930-0601

Paper Adventures, 901 South 5th St., Milwaukee, WI 53204

Pebbles Inc., www.pebblesinc.com

Plaid/All Night Media, 3225 Westech Dr., Norcross, GA 30092

PM Designs, 565 W. Lambert Unit B, Brea, CA 92821, (888) 595-2887, www.puzzlemates.com

Provo Craft/Sizzix, mail-order source: Creative Express, 295 W. Center St., Provo, UT 84601-4436

Ranger Industries Inc., 15 Park Rd., Tinton Falls, NJ 07724

Royal & Langnickel, www.royalbrush.com

Rubber Stamp Ave., P.O. Box 8178, Medford, OR 97504, (541) 665-9981

Designer & Project Index